LINNAEUS

LINNAEUS

HEINZ GOERKE

Translated from the German
by DENVER LINDLEY

CHARLES SCRIBNER'S SONS
New York

Contents

Part Two: CAREER AND INFLUENCE

Illustrations

Preface

The German publisher's invitation to write a biography of Linnaeus raised the question of whether a medical historian would have all the necessary qualifications. The consideration that Linnaeus had been professor of medicine at Uppsala and that his achievements in the natural sciences must take into account his work as a physician may at least partially justify my acceptance of the assignment. I must beg indulgence, however, if in certain passages the doctor in Linnaeus is perhaps too heavily stressed and if in others he is presented simply as a doctor. Whether this makes for an improvement in the portrait only the reader can judge—most readily, no doubt, by comparison with other biographies of Linnaeus.

Hardly any other eighteenth-century scholar left behind as much autobiographical material as Linnaeus did. And there is certainly no other naturalist whose life and work have been so often and so thoroughly appraised or subjected to so many individual studies. The wealth of available material both increases and decreases the difficulty of presenting his life. The time for a truly comprehensive biography has clearly not yet come. Much material is still unedited and unpublished, and some has appeared only in part, as, for instance, the collections of letters. Although the Swedish Linnaean Society has edited Linnaeus's more important writings, subsidized the publication of separate works, and also uncovered new material, these publications have been almost without exception in Swedish.

In preparing this book, I have separated the external facts of Linnaeus's life from the description of his scientific work. I did so in order to make use of his autobiographical writings in Part One and thus show something of his life and character. The account of his scientific work in Part Two, on the other hand, has been done along methodical and objective lines. Even though for Linnaeus botany was the beloved science *(scientia amabilis)* and his name is linked with the history and the present of this science, I have considered it proper to evaluate his achievements as the taxonomist of botany from the point of view of method. Although I have intentionally shaped this biography of Linnaeus differently from those previously published, there were models available, from Afzelius to Malmeström's latest work, that have inspired and helped me. Any study of Linnaeus must, in addition to determining his scientific and historical importance, maintain an awareness of his meaning for Sweden. My close personal associations in that country and my residence there for a number of years, plus the fact that for more than a decade I have been occupied with the history of Scandinavian science, made the task especially attractive to me.

To the editor and the publisher of the German edition go my heartfelt thanks for the great understanding and patience with which my wishes have been carried out. With deep gratitude I recall the constant helpfulness and expert knowledge of the veteran secretary of the Swedish Linnaean Society, library director Dr. Arvid Hjalmar Uggla (Uppsala), who to my great regret did not live to see the completion of this biography. In numerous letters and conversations Dr. Telemak Fredbärj (Stockholm), the outstanding authority on Linnaeus and the celebrated editor of *Selected Transactions,* has given me a wealth of valuable suggestions and important hints. To Dr. Birger Strandell (Stockholm), a successor to

Linnaeus and the owner of the largest private collection of Linnaeus's writings, I owe the outstanding experience of having had in my own hands even the rarest of Linnaeus's works in their original editions. I have been variously assisted by numerous other Swedish colleagues, among them Dr. Wolfram Kock (Stockholm), and by several great libraries, in particular the University Library in Lund. In conclusion I must mention with especial praise the activities of the Swedish Linnaean Society in preserving and maintaining the memorials in Stenbrohult, Uppsala, and Hammarby. Much in the life and writings of Linnaeus would have remained obscure and incomprehensible to me had I not been able to pay repeated visits to these places.

LINNAEUS

Introduction

Events and Temper of Linnaeus's Times

Carolus Linnaeus's lifetime, 1707–1778, spanned nearly three-quarters of the eventful eighteenth century. In the year of his birth, Charles XII, the twenty-five-year-old king of Sweden, was in Saxony with an army of 40,000 men; in the late summer he marched eastward. Two years later he was decisively defeated by the Russians at Poltava. Charles himself, with his trusted intimates, found refuge in Turkey. After a famous ride straight across Europe—more than 1200 miles in fifteen days—he reached Stralsund in November 1714. A year later, on November 30, during a campaign against Norway, he was killed in front of the citadel at Fredrikshald. Whether he was killed by a stray bullet or was assassinated by one of the hangers-on of his brother-in-law, Crown Prince Frederick of Hesse, will probably never be known. Subsequently Sweden lost the Baltic provinces, lower Pomerania south of the Peene, Bremen, and Verden. Exhausted by war, the nation suffered internal political disruption, and the executive power fell more and more into the hands of the estates. Charles XII's sister, Ulrica Eleonora, succeeded him, but in 1720 she renounced the throne in favor of her husband, who became Frederick I of Sweden, while retaining the title of

Landgrave of Hesse-Kassel. Under him the Swedish crown lost even more of its political influence, though the country recuperated with surprising rapidity from the severe economic consequences of the war. Commerce in iron and lumber reached new heights and helped the economic revival, but foreign policy became involved in a violent conflict between the two leading groups in Parliament, the pro-French party, the "Hats" and the pro-Russian "Caps." In a war against Russia Sweden lost parts of Finland in 1743. At the instigation of the victor, Adolphus Frederick of the house of Holstein-Gottorp was named Crown Prince of Sweden and ascended the throne in 1751. His marriage to Louisa Ulrica, the younger sister of Frederick the Great of Prussia, was arranged for reasons of state. As king, Adolphus Frederick had even less influence in internal affairs than his predecessor, and his wife's attempt to wield political power also failed. She was far more successful, however, in her efforts to advance the arts and sciences. The gifted son of Adolphus Frederick and Louisa Ulrica came to the throne in 1771 as Gustavus III, and the following year he restored absolute power to the crown through a coup d'état. The influence of the nobility and the estates was curtailed, the rights of the peasants were widened, and torture was abolished. Gustavus III was assassinated by political opponents on March 16, 1792, at the opera ball in Stockholm.

Since the end of the Middle Ages Uppsala had played an outstanding role as the center of Swedish intellectual life and as the residence of its highest ecclesiastical dignitaries. The university founded there in 1477 was for almost two centuries the only institution of higher learning in the Swedish homeland. Then in the year 1668 a second university was founded in the city of Lund in southern Sweden, primarily to attach the provinces acquired in 1658 more firmly to Sweden by providing the sons of these formerly Danish territories with a university of their own, but also in the hope of counteracting their tendency to prefer to study in Copenhagen. However, although these two universities were available in Sweden at the turn of the eighteenth century, many young Swedes completed the greater part of their studies abroad, especially in Dutch universities. In the case of medical students this can be explained by the requirement in the royal decree of 1688 that all medical students wishing to practice in Sweden must pass an examination before the College of Medicine in Stockholm. The medical faculties at Uppsala and Lund saw this as a curtailment of their prerogatives, stopped bestowing the M.D. degree, and thereafter preferred that their students complete their studies abroad. Only after the royal edict of 1737 took away from the College of Medicine the sole right to examine medical students from home universities did this situation change.

In the last third of the seventeenth century and the first quarter of the eighteenth, the foundations of a specifically Swedish science of medicine had already been laid down. Among the leading medical scholars of the country Olof Rudbeck the elder (1630–1702) is prominent especially for his anatomical and botanical labors, the arrangement of a botanical garden (1655), and the Anatomical Theater (1662–1663) in Uppsala. Together with him, Petrus Hoffvenius (1630–1682), Urban Hjärne (1641–1742), a student of Rudbeck and Hoffvenius, and Johan von Hoorn (1662–1724), who performed meritorious services in the field of gynecology, founded an independent school of medicine in Sweden.

The intellectual currents that swept the European continent in the eighteenth century reached Sweden through the younger academic generation's studies abroad and the often fruitful contacts of Swedish scholars with their colleagues in other European countries. Naturally enough, relations were especially close with the southern Baltic provinces, which were still partially under Swedish sovereignty and with the Protestant universities in Germany. The ideas of the Enlightenment were relatively late in penetrating into Sweden. Originating in England around the middle of the seventeenth century, these ideas had spread by way of Holland across the continent, had taken definitive form in France, and from there had swept across the rest of Europe and beyond. About 1730 Cartesianism, which had hitherto been the prevailing philosophy in Uppsala, began to yield to the teachings of the Enlightenment in the form of the rationalistic system of the German philosopher Christian von Wolff (1679–1754) championed especially by the mathematician Samuel Klingenstjerna and the philosophy professor and theologian Petrus Ullén.

To understand Linnaeus and his influence on his time, an influence that went substantially beyond his own fields of natural science and medicine and made his name familiar to princes as well as to people uninterested in science, his contemporaries must be considered. A survey of the great men whose careers were concurrent with that of Linnaeus, those whose later life overlaps his early years, and those who were born when he was completing his scientific work reveals a fascinating range of political, cultural, and scientific happenings.

A few European monarchs attempted to meet the challenge of the times by acting as representatives of enlightened absolutism. In Russia Peter the Great and Catherine II, born a princess of Anhalt-Zerbst and Czarina from 1762 to 1796, developed their country into a great European power. Frederick the Great who reigned from 1740 to 1786 and whose success at "inner colonization" was no less than his military accomplishments, established the power status of Prussia. The Holy Roman Emperor Joseph II, son of Frederick's opponent the Archduchess Maria Theresa of Austria and co-regent with her from 1765 until her death in 1780, acquired through a series of reform measures the reputation of being a humanitarian monarch, despite the fact that he brought upon his country several grave domestic and foreign crises. From 1715 to 1774 Louis XV was king of France; the powerful influence of his mistress Madame de Pompadour prevailed from 1743 to 1764. The first Hanoverian King of England, George I, ascended the throne in 1714; he was succeeded in 1727 by his son, George II. After the latter's death in 1760, his grandson George Wilhelm Frederick, the first member of this dynasty to be born in England, took the throne as George III.

The great wars of the eighteenth century, precipitated mostly by quarrels over succession, not only brought changes in the balance of power but also had a considerable importance in cultural matters. Among them were the Northern War (1700–1721), the War of the Spanish Succession (1701–1714), the War of the Austrian Succession (1740–1748), the Seven Years' War (1756–1763), and the various Russo-Turkish wars. The American colonies' War of Independence (1775–1783) is of special significance, since the inauguration of George Washington (born in 1732) as President of the United States in 1789 marked the first appearance of a state governed in accordance with the principles of a modern constitution.

Philosophy had such a powerful influence on the whole intellectual life of the eighteenth century that the names of at least the leading figures must be mentioned. Among the Germans, the activities of Gottfried Wilhelm von Leibniz (1646–1716) and of his follower Christian von Wolff fall at least partially within Linnaeus's lifetime. The critic and dramatist Gotthold Ephraim Lessing (1729–1781)was his contemporary; Lessing's religious philosophy was deistic and critical of revelation. Another contemporary was Immanuel Kant (1714–1804) with whom the defeat of rationalism began. The French philosophical writers Voltaire and Jean-Jacques Rousseau both died in the same year as Linnaeus. Still another contemporary was Linnaeus's fellow countryman Emanuel Swedenborg (1688–1772), versatile scholar, natural philosopher, and religious writer.

The Italian playwright Carlo Goldoni was born in the same year as Linnaeus. When Linnaeus died, Johann Wolfgang von Goethe was twenty-eight years old, and Friedrich Schiller, at eighteen, was studying to be an army doctor in the Karlsschule in Stuttgart. In the field of music, Johann Sebastian Bach died in 1750, Georg Friedrich Handel nine years later. Wolfgang Amadeus Mozart was born in 1756 and Ludwig van Beethoven in 1770.

In the areas of natural science and medicine many figures will be encountered in the story of Linnaeus's life and work, since he was in personal contact with a great number of the most important naturalists and doctors of his time. These included Hermann Boerhaave (1668–1739), known as *Praeceptor totius Europae* [teacher of all Europe], and Albrecht von Haller (1708–1777), the polymath and founder of experimental physiology. The two great systematizers at Halle, Friedrich Hoffmann (1660–1742) and Ernst Georg Stahl (1660–1734), made a lasting impact on medicine, while in 1759 Caspar Friedrich Wolff (1733–1794) published his *Theoria generationis* [Theory of Evolution]. In 1761 appeared *De sedibus et causis morborum* [Concerning the Location and Causes of Diseases], by the Italian physician Giovanni Battista Morgagni (1682–1771), and the Austrian Leopold Auenbrugger (1722–1809) introduced the technique of percussion, the value and use of which were not generally recognized until six decades later. Five years before Linnaeus's death the physician to King Christian VII of Denmark and powerful statesman Johann Friedrich von Struensee, who had been born in Halle in 1737, died on the scaffold. Another victim of violence was the Swiss-born doctor Jean Paul Marat (1743–1793), the "friend of the people" who became the most hated man of the French Revolution. In 1752 Benjamin Franklin (1706–1790) invented the lightning rod. In 1765 James Watt (1736–1819) invented the first practical steam engine. Oxygen was discovered by Carl Wilhelm Scheele (1742–1786) in Uppsala in 1771, the year that Joseph Priestley (1733–1804) made the same discovery in England.

Any orientation survey of the political, intellectual, and cultural background of Linnaeus's life must mention mathematics, for this field was essential to the thinking of the period. Daniel Bernoulli (1700–1782), a scion of the famous Basel family, physician and professor of anatomy and botany, later of physics, was co-founder of mathematical physics. The versatile and highly creative mathematician and physicist Leonhard Euler (1707–1783) was born, like Bernoulli, in Basel. He went to St. Petersburg in 1730 and died there in 1783; from 1744 to 1776 he was active in the Berlin Academy of Sciences. For both these Basel scholars, mathematics, the epitome of sovereign reason for the men of the Enlightenment, was the favorite subject of study. But Linnaeus too was representative in his fashion of this tendency of the age. Through talent and insight, he became the systematizer of nature. The ground had been well prepared for his work.

Part One

THE MAN

1

Family and Childhood

In the city of Stavanger in southern Norway in 1622 Johanne Pedersdotter, wife of the burgess Simon Jacobson Schee, was burned as a witch. She left behind her a ten-year-old son, Jörgen Simonson Schee, who grew up to become a clergyman. In 1640 he was given the parish of Visseltofta in Skåne, now the southernmost part of Sweden but at that time, together with Norway, still under Danish rule. It did not become part of Sweden until 1658.

In Stenbrohult, a few miles from Visseltofta, Pedrus Broderson had been given the incumbency of his father-in-law's parish in 1622. In 1687 his son Samuel married Maria Schee, the parson's daughter from Visseltofta, and a year later, after her father's death, took over the parish. The first child in this parson's family, Christina Broderson, the mother of Linnaeus, was born in 1688.

In 1703 parson Samuel Broderson in Stenbrohult asked the cathedral chapter to fill the long-vacant position of chaplain in his parish. They sent him a twenty-nine-year-old theological student, Nils Ingemarsson Linnaeus, a farmer's son from a neighboring district, one of the poorest in Småland. The young assistant to the parson quickly won the liking of the congregation and of his superior but found his own special interest in the parson's daughter. Barely two years later he was named assistant minister of the congregation and was given as residence the nearby small farm of Råshult. On March 6, 1705, he married Christina Broderson, and shortly thereafter they moved into the farmhouse. There, in the night of May 22, 1707,* a son was born who was named Carl after the reigning king.

"*Potest e casa vir magnus exire* [A great man can come forth from a cabin]" was inscribed by Carl Linnaeus at the head of one of his autobiographical essays. Of his birth he wrote: "It was the fairest time of spring when the cuckoo is heralding summer, between the unfolding of the leaf and the opening of the blossom."[1] The fact that he came into the world at the time of year when nature shows its most enchanting aspect in his homeland was later regarded by Linnaeus as symbolic of a divine mission to explore nature and classify it in accordance with its creator's plan.

In 1709 Nils Linnaeus was appointed regular minister of the congregation as successor to his father-in-law. He then moved into the parsonage at Stenbrohult close by the church, and it was there that his son passed his childhood and youth.

The house where Linnaeus was born and the church, only a ten-minute walk from it, lie in a wholly typical Swedish landscape. The great lake, Möckeln, with its bay and islands is nearby. Gentle hills and steep slopes are adorned with flowers; there are wide meadows and forests of deciduous trees mixed with conifers. In many places granite thrusts up from the fields; boulders are scattered all about. These childhood scenes remained radiant in Linnaeus's mind, and to him no other landscape in all his native land could compare with the country around Stenbrohult.

Much has been written about the influence of his parents' lives on Linnaeus's inclinations and future life work. A Swed-

* The Gregorian calendar was introduced into Sweden in the year 1753. The adjustment was made on February 17, which was followed by March 1. The dates in this book before that day are given in the "old style" of the Julian calendar.

ish parsonage in the eighteenth century was no luxurious dwelling; only through thrift and diligence was it possible to raise the often large numbers of children and provide schooling for the boys. Linnaeus's parents were markedly different from each other in personality and in character. "He was of a very gentle, calm, and kindly disposition; she was shrewd, lively, and diligent."[2]

Nils, the father, was remarkably sensitive to the beauties of nature, especially of vegetation. The name Linnaeus, which he adopted when he began his theological studies, is symbolic of this. A tall linden tree that stood close to his father's farmhouse prompted him to call himself Linnaeus, from the tree's Swedish name, *lind*. A generation earlier, according to tradition, the same tree had inspired one of his mother's brothers to choose the family name Tiliander, from the Latin name for the linden tree. This uncle, Sven Tiliander, was also a parson, and very likely it was he who awakened young Nils to the pleasures of collecting plants and planning a garden around his house. As a young man Sven had been household chaplain to the Swedish governor general, Henrik Horn, in Bremen, and he probably had the well-tended gardens of that city in mind when, to the great astonishment of his congregation, he adorned his parsonage garden with rare flowers and plants. Nils Linnaeus followed his uncle's example when he moved into the chaplain's small house in Råshult. He spent every free hour in his garden, transplanted rare and beautiful plants from around the neighborhood and many from his uncle's garden. The young parson's pleasure in his hobby was shared by his wife, who had previously never even seen a proper flower garden. Linnaeus firmly believed that his career as a botanist was predestined; years later he attributed it to his mother's preferring to spend her time in the beautiful parsonage garden when she was carrying him.

Of the garden's place in his early life, Linnaeus wrote: "This as yet only son was, as it were, educated by his father in the garden. The latter designed, as soon as he became parson in Stenbrohult, one of the finest gardens in the whole province, carefully selecting trees and rare flowers, and whenever he was free from the duties of his office spent his leisure there."³ Linnaeus's father taught his first-born the names of the plants in the garden and aroused the boy's interest in botany very early. When the father went on his pastoral rounds, the boy often accompanied him, and everywhere they would find new bushes and flowers. His mother was not too pleased at this inclination on the part of her son, for the parents had always agreed that the child should some day become a parson.

In addition to training in botany, Nils gave his son preliminary grounding in reading and writing. When the boy was seven years old a tutor was hired, but he proved to be totally uninterested in teaching a child. Three years later little Carl was admitted to the elementary school in Växjö. There "crude teachers endeavored to instill in the children a liking for the sciences with such crude methods that it made their hair stand on end."⁴ At this point Carl lost the last vestige of interest in formal education. Once more for a short time he had a private tutor, who later married his sister. But this man, though he had a kindly, mild disposition, also failed to make the boy a good student.

In 1724, Carl, then seventeen, entered the secondary school in Växjö. In the curriculum, essentially intended "to prepare useful material for the ministry,"⁵ he showed a strikingly uneven interest. In mathematics and physics he was among the best students; in the remaining subjects, including rhetoric, metaphysics, ethics, Greek, Hebrew, and theology, he was one of the worst. But botany was his real love. He had managed to acquire a few well-known books about plants; he quickly mastered their contents but even as a schoolboy recognized their shortcomings. His teachers and schoolmates were aware of this special interest, and he is said to have been jestingly called "the little botanist."

About two years later, when Nils Linnaeus visited the school in Växjö to consult the teachers about the progress and abilities of his son, he was told that the boy ought to learn a trade since he was not suited to higher education. But before Nils returned home he went to see the provincial doctor in Växjö on a medical matter. The doctor, Johan Rothman, as was the custom at that time, also taught the natural sciences at the secondary school. During the consultation the conversation came around to Carl's unsuccessful career at school. Rothman remarked on the boy's unusual talent for natural science and pleaded that the father under no circumstances allow his son to miss the following school year; he volunteered to give the boy every possible assistance. He emphatically warned Nils against forcing the boy into the study of theology.

Johan Rothman kept his word. In a spirit of fatherly friendship he assisted Carl, instructing him privately in physiology and botany and advancing him so successfully that, at the end of the following year, Carl received a certificate of completion of the school course. Without the help of this benefactor Linnaeus might well have become merely a tailor or cobbler with a love for flowers.

2

Studies at Lund and Uppsala

Carl's enthusiasm for his courses in science and medicine at Växjö was so great that, in spite of his boredom with the general curriculum, he was given an opportunity to continue his education. On August 17, 1727, he arrived in Lund in southern Sweden and two days later matriculated at the university. He found lodgings in the house of Kilian Stobaeus, a doctor and lecturer in medicine who rented him a room for a small sum. Stobaeus was outwardly unprepossessing. He limped as a result of a childhood attack of tuberculosis of the hip; he had the use of only one eye, was frequently sick, and often suffered from migraine headaches. He had a large natural-science collection, which he was constantly increasing by collecting and trading, and an unusually extensive herbarium.

Linnaeus soon found that around Lund, especially on the nearby Baltic coast, there were many plants he had never seen before. He spent days on excursions to enlarge his herbarium, but he lacked the books necessary to continue his botanical studies as Johan Rothman had recommended when he left Växjö. However, he soon made friends with a student from Lausitz, David Samuel Koulas, who was Stobaeus's secretary and had the run of his library. Through Koulas,

Linnaeus could borrow books without Stobaeus's knowledge, working his way through them in his room by candlelight.

One night, Linnaeus reported in his autobiography, Stobaeus appeared in his roomer's quarters at one-thirty and found him reading at a table piled with books from his own library. Linnaeus had to confess how he had obtained them, but there was an unexpected outcome. The satisfaction every real scholar feels on encountering genuine intellectual hunger conquered Stobaeus's indignation. He not only forgave the clandestine borrowing of his books but the next morning gave Linnaeus permission to take books from his library at will, to attend his lectures without a fee, and to have his meals at the house without charge. Thereafter Linnaeus was allowed to accompany Stobaeus on his sick calls. "I am gratefully indebted to this gentleman for as long as I live on account of the affection he felt for me, for he loved me not as a student but rather as his son."[1]

In Lund young Linnaeus also had the opportunity to become acquainted with mineralogy. Stobaeus's natural-science collection included a great many stones and fossils, illustrative material of remarkable extent and variety. From Stobaeus Linnaeus also learned a good deal of practical medicine. The only chair in medicine at Lund was occupied by Johan Jakob Döbel, who had little influence on Linnaeus or the other students at the university. He was regional doctor for Skåne, spa physician in Ramlösa, and holder of various nonmedical posts and consequently had scarcely any time to spend on teaching.

In the course of a botanical excursion in the summer of 1728 young Linnaeus fell ill as a result of a large purulent inflammation on his arm, presumably caused by an insect bite. A surgeon had to open the sore, and for many weeks Linnaeus was too sick to undertake the journey home. When he finally reached his father's parsonage, his recuperation was rapid, and his joy in botany and arranging the herbarium returned. It was then that his mother realized how strong was her son's bent toward natural science, and especially botany, and finally ceased to hope that the study of medicine, which he had already begun, might be traded for that of theology. At this point Rothman advised that Linnaeus discontinue his studies at Lund and go instead to Uppsala, where the great library, the Botanical Garden, and the possibility of getting a scholarship promised a much more favorable educational future.

With a hundred talers in his pocket Linnaeus left for Uppsala, arriving on September 5, 1728, at the oldest university in Sweden. The name Uppsala has ever since been linked with his own throughout the world.

The medical faculty at Uppsala consisted at this time of Olof Rudbeck the younger, son of the famous rector of the university, and Lars Roberg. Rudbeck, who taught anatomy and botany, had earned a fine reputation through his studies of birds native to Sweden. His lectures on this subject were popular, and Linnaeus was among his attentive listeners. Roberg, who taught theoretical and practical medicine, was not nearly so well thought of.

Linnaeus's money for study did not last long, and he was soon facing the future with serious anxiety. However, another happy accident again provided him with a fatherly friend and benefactor. Linnaeus was a constant visitor to the Botanical Garden in Uppsala, which, though unkempt through neglect, contained many plants hitherto unknown to him, especially some not native to Sweden. One day as he was looking about in this garden, an elderly gentleman in clerical attire noticed his obvious interest. They fell into conversation, and the gentleman was amazed to discover that Linnaeus had a sound knowledge of botany and a particularly impressive command of the nomenclature of plants according to the system devised by the French botanist Joseph Pitton de Tournefort (1656–1708). The elderly gentleman was Olof Celsius, a professor of theology and a highly versatile scholar, who at this time had taken up botany as a hobby, with special interest in plants mentioned in the Bible. Celsius took Linnaeus home for a further talk and later went to see his herbarium. After a few days he had become so interested in the young man that he gave him a room in his house and a place at his table. Thus Linnaeus's financial problems were solved; he had found in Uppsala another Stobaeus. He also formed a close friendship with one of his fellow students, Peter Artedi, barely two years his senior.

Shortly before Linnaeus's arrival in Uppsala Nils Rosén had been appointed assistant lecturer in medicine, but the appointment was contingent on a period of study at various universities on the continent to advance his education and experience in medicine, and Rosén had left Uppsala for this purpose. During his three-year absence a substitute was appointed whose teaching methods were not popular with the students. Then, in 1730, when the retirement of the aged Rudbeck was being considered on condition that he name a qualified substitute, the faculty appointed Linnaeus professor of botany.

Giving a professorship to a student in his third year was highly unusual and did not meet with unanimous faculty approval; Lars Roberg, who held the other professorship in medicine, withheld his vote because of serious doubts. Rudbeck, however, had formed an altogether favorable impression of Linnaeus, especially on account of his little essay *Praeludia sponsaliorum plantarum* [Prelude to the Betrothals of Plants], which had appeared on New Year's Day, 1730, with a dedication to Olof Celsius. In this essay Linnaeus simply yet poetically presented the doctrine of the sexuality of plants. The view that the stamens and pistils of plants are specifically sexual organs had been advanced by a few botanists—the Englishman Nehemiah Grew (1641–1711), the German Rudolph Jacob Camerarius (1665–1721), and the Frenchman Sébastien Vaillant (1669–1721)—but had received little support. Linnaeus's essay, although it was only a small work by an unknown medical student, aroused so much respect throughout Uppsala that Rudbeck was able to put through Linnaeus's appointment. From the beginning of 1730 Linnaeus gave lectures and conducted excursions in the Botanical Garden. About the same time he became resident tutor to Rudbeck's children.

Through Rudbeck Linnaeus had also been given supervision of the Botanical Garden. With the assistance of the gardener, he began to acquire numerous rare plants from other gardens and from the surrounding countryside, and he designed and planted new flower beds. Soon the students were coming to Linnaeus for private lectures, but no matter how great the calls on his time, he did not neglect his own scientific work. Now that he had unlimited access to Rudbeck's library, even richer in botanical works than that of Olof Celsius, he could make a start with the literary execution of what he himself described as the "reformation of botany." He worked unceasingly, completing several manuscripts which were not printed until later. The most important parts of *Bibliotheca botanica* [Botanical Dictionary], *Classes plantarum* [Classes of Plants], *Critica botanica* [Botanical Criticism] and *Genera plantarum* [Genera of Plants] belong to this period.

In 1731 Nils Rosén returned to Uppsala from his trip abroad. Fresh from his experiences at the universities on the continent, he took up his teaching duties at Uppsala and, moreover, soon became the most sought-after doctor in the city, for there had been no qualified practitioner since Roberg and Rudbeck had almost completely given up their practices. A tense situation promptly developed between Rosén and Linnaeus. Rosén clearly had the advantage. After he received his appointment for the anatomy lectures, he set to work to get the botany lectures as well; that is, he coveted both subjects of Rudbeck's professorship. Rudbeck himself, however, prevented the transfer of the botany courses, obviously out of a conviction that the scientific interests and accomplishments of Linnaeus in that subject were far greater than Rosén's. Although Rosén pulled every string, and even attempted personally to persuade Linnaeus to give up his teaching assignment, the situation remained unchanged, and years later Linnaeus was still uttering harsh words about Rosén. At about this time disagreements occurred in Rudbeck's household which resulted in Linnaeus's losing his benefactor's confidence and having to find another place to live.

Rudbeck had often talked about the rare flora and fauna in Lapland and had been so enthusiastic about his trip through this northernmost Swedish province that Linnaeus had a great desire to go there himself. Very likely Linnaeus was also desirous of leaving Uppsala for a time and trying for an achievement which his rival would not be able to match. By royal decree the Royal Society of Science in Uppsala had been entrusted with carrying out a research expedition through Lapland, and because of this Linnaeus was able to get financial support for the trip. He did, however, have to work to get the funds, as is evident from his presenting to the society on December 15, 1731, a request for a grant of 600 copper talers. He pointed out that Lapland was a region "that had been very widely mentioned by the oldest poets and historians, either with praise or scorn. And now after all Europe and almost the whole world has been investigated, as far as the natural sciences are concerned, Lapland still lies almost as if shrouded in a state of darkest barbarism. . . ."[2] He expressed the hope that in Lapland, more than anywhere else in the world, there would be the opportunity for unusual discoveries and observations in all three of nature's kingdoms. His application gave reasons why he himself was the right person for this journey of discovery, pointing out that he was a citizen of Sweden, healthy, indefatigable, had no permanent employment, was unmarried, and was both a naturalist and a doctor. He especially emphasized that, since he was a bachelor, he could cross raging torrents on rafts without having to worry about wife and children. The society acknowledged his application but did not reach a decision. Linnaeus kept reminding those concerned, and finally on April 15, 1732, he was granted 400 copper talers for traveling expenses. The money was paid him eleven days later by the society's secretary, Anders Celsius, a nephew of Olof Celsius.

On May 12 Linnaeus began his long journey. For five months he studied the country and the people in the north of Sweden, collected specimens, made drawings, encountered hardship and danger, but was able thereby to enrich substantially his personal knowledge in all branches of natural science. In October he returned to Uppsala and a few weeks later rendered an account of his findings, discoveries, observations, and results before the Royal Society of Sciences.

Linnaeus resumed lecturing but with only meager returns. His chief source of funds was a scholarship that he received early in 1732 and after his return from Lapland. Before that trip his stay at Uppsala had been financed by royal stipends in various amounts, which, together with assistance from Celsius and Rudbeck, had allowed him to continue his studies. But now the rivalry of Rosén posed a threat; in Linnaeus's autobiographical notes one can detect the bitterness with which he watched Rosén's successful academic and social career. Linnaeus even reports that Rosén, through requests and later through threats, secured the loan of the manuscript of his botanical lectures. When he discovered that copies were being made, he had to insist with considerable force that the manuscript be returned.

In December 1733 Linnaeus took a short trip to the province of Dalecarlia [now Kopparberg] to examine the mines and smelters there; his interest in mineralogy had been aroused in Lapland, and in Dalecarlia he encountered formations hitherto unknown to him. The judiciousness of his recorded observations and his disregard of danger and physical exertion, when there was a chance of finding something that had escaped other observers, are obvious in his report of the journey. For example, he went down into a copper mine at Falun to watch the miners at work. What he saw there underground was "the replica of hell."

In Falun he became acquainted with Nils Reuterholm, the provincial governor of Dalecarlia, who was most interested in the reports of his journey and urged him to make another trip through the more remote parts of the province at Reuterholm's expense. Returning to Uppsala, Linnaeus to his great distress was confronted with further academic advances by Rosén which made his own prospects as unfavorable as possible. He therefore took advantage of Reuterholm's offer and undertook the journey through Dalecarlia. He went first to Falun where he was joined by a group of traveling companions, young people interested in natural science. The trip lasted six weeks and covered all parts of the province, as well as some Norwegian territory.

In the latter part of August Linnaeus returned to Falun,

where he was the guest of the governor. In this household Linnaeus met Johan Browallius, family chaplain and tutor, and they became friends. Later Browallius was to be professor and bishop in Åbo. Linnaeus gave Browallius lessons in mineralogy and botany, sessions which were also attended by other interested citizens of Falun. He soon felt exceptionally at home in this mountain city, especially since he was called upon more and more frequently for medical services.

During this period he had time to discuss his future prospects with Browallius, and it became clear to him that there could be no successful continuation of his career unless he took an M.D. degree. To do so would require study abroad, since the Swedish universities, for reasons explained earlier, were giving very few medical degrees at this time. Browallius proposed a plan—Linnaeus should look about for a rich wife "who could first make him happy and then he her." In his autobiography Linnaeus indicates that he quite approved of the suggestion, but he is careful not to admit that he acted on Browallius's advice. Nevertheless, he became friends with the municipal doctor in Falun, Johan Moraeus, a wealthy man, and before long asked for the hand of Moraeus's eldest daughter, "with whom he already had an agreement."

3

Sojourn in Holland

Whether or not Linnaeus's future father-in-law took part in financing his educational journey is nowhere indicated. However, Linnaeus does mention in his travel notes that he considered it important to choose a traveling companion who would help with the expenses. The son of a mine inspector in Falun, Clas Sohlberg, a medical student, seemed to meet this requirement, since his father promised to contribute 300 copper talers yearly. But when the time for departure came, there was no more talk of the 300 copper talers. Linnaeus evidently was given a small sum to keep him quiet about the whole affair. Preparations had been completed, he had received money and supplies from various sources, and so he had to proceed with the journey. With only 60 silver talers in his pocket, and young Sohlberg tagging along, Linnaeus started off in the firm belief that this time too the Lord God could be trusted not to leave him in the lurch.

This very important year of Linnaeus's life, 1735, can be reconstructed in more complete detail than any other, thanks to the almost daily entries in his pocket diary.[1]

On January 22 Linnaeus, wishing to be formally engaged to Sarah Elisabeth Moraea, gave her a ring; next day it was handed back to him by her mother. The engagement was nevertheless formed, and when Linnaeus left Falun at the end of February Doctor Moraeus had agreed to the three-year absence of his future son-in-law, and his daughter was bound by a written pledge.

By way of Nora and Örebo the students traveled southward along the ancient trade route and after a three-week trip arrived in Växjö, scene of Linnaeus's school days. Here they spent a number of days in the company of his former teacher Johan Rothman. Then Linnaeus visited the parsonage in Stenbrohult for three weeks; his aged father was living there alone after his wife's death.

On April 22 Linnaeus and Sohlberg embarked at Hälsingborg on the Lübeck sailing vessel *Der reisende Tobias* and landed on April 26 in Travemünde. "Here it was magnificent summer." With rapture Linnaeus inspected the well-tended gardens and fields, a landscape he had heard much about but never before seen. After a brief stopover in Lübeck, still an important city for Swedish relations with the mainland, though by no means as much so as in the Middle Ages, they continued their journey on April 28, traveling by stagecoach to Hamburg.

Linnaeus already had a connection in that city through his correspondence with Johann Peter Kohl. Kohl had been professor of ecclesiastical history in St. Petersburg from 1725 to 1728. He had been expelled from Russia because of too intimate relations with Princess Elizabeth (later Czarina), but he had been granted a lifetime pension and was living as a private scholar in Hamburg. As the editor of the *Hamburgische Berichte für gelehrte Sachen* [Hamburg Reports on Scholarly Affairs], Kohl possessed widespread connections. Ever since 1732 he had been publishing various items about Linnaeus, his work, and his travels in Sweden. The Linnaeus expert Felix Bryk has been able to prove that these notes were written by Linnaeus himself and that Kohl received them through the agency of Christian Nettelbladt, a professor at Greifswald who had a high opinion of Linnaeus. Because of these short items in Kohl's journal, Linnaeus was already known, by name at least, in scholarly circles on the continent. Linnaeus remained in Hamburg for almost three weeks and met Kohl many times. He was also able to visit the library of the director of the city school, where books "lined the walls from floor to ceiling," and he met the botanist Johann Heinrich Spreckelsen, whose garden and collection of natural-history specimens he mentions appreciatively in his diary. The two students also tried to get a look at as many of the sights of this great city as possible. Then on May 12 they boarded a Hamburg sailing freighter at Altona, then a Danish city, and drifted down the Elbe with the tide. After a voyage that was stormy, especially between the continent and the Frisian Islands and across the Zuider Zee, they reached Amsterdam on June 2.

Linnaeus's stay in Holland turned out to be of crucial importance for his academic career and the general influence he later exerted. There he found advancement and understanding to an extent impossible in his native country. Holland at this time was blossoming in every way. Though the country was no longer in its heyday—its golden seventeenth century was past—nevertheless, for the visitor from Sweden, a country weakened and impoverished by war, conditions in Holland's realm of science were truly marvelous. Linnaeus made use of his educational opportunities as few people have ever done. He went to great lengths to cultivate important and influential men; he exerted himself to see museums, collections, and gardens. On the very first day in Amsterdam he visited the Medical Garden. Next day he paid a courtesy call on Johannes Burmann, a professor of botany with whom he later came to be on very friendly terms, and on the following day he inspected the famous collection of natural-history specimens belonging to the resident German pharmacist Albert Seba.

The two students then traveled by ship to Harderwijk, where the university, though of no great consequence in itself, was a favorite with Swedish students of the eighteenth century for taking an M.D. The reason for this, if not especially creditable, is easily understood: the degree could be acquired rapidly and at relatively little expense. Linnaeus must certainly have gone to Harderwijk on the advice of

Johan Rothman, who had taken his own degree there. Nils Rosén too had received his diploma at Harderwijk.

The day after his arrival Linnaeus passed the medical examination, and on the very next day the director of the university granted him permission to print his dissertation, which he had already written in Sweden: *Hypothesis nova de febrium intermittentium causa* [A New Theory concerning the Cause of Intermittent Fevers]. Four days later, on June 12, 1735, he was allowed to defend this thesis in a formal disputation. The university's disputation rostrum, a richly ornamented double pulpit of wood in baroque style, adorned with the eagles of the House of Orange and the lion of the City of Harderwijk, is still preserved in the city museum, though the university itself was closed in 1811. It was customary for the sponsor, in this case the rector of the university, Johan de Gorter, to sit in the upper chair of the double rostrum, and it was Gorter who, after due completion of the disputation, handed Linnaeus his doctor's diploma, a document which is now in the Linnaeus Museum in Uppsala.

Happy that he had achieved the real object of his journey so quickly, Linnaeus left Harderwijk on the following day. By way of Amsterdam and Haarlem he traveled to Leyden, the oldest university city in Holland and the true cultural center of the country. Presumably he had not yet found a suitable opportunity for the trip home and had followed Sohlberg, who was in a better position financially and who planned to continue his studies in Leyden. Linnaeus at once enrolled at the university as an auditor, paid a call on the professor of botany, Adrian van Royen, and made the acquaintance of the botanist and physician Johan Friederich Gronovius. In his autobiography Linnaeus described Gronovius as the most intellectually inquisitive Dutchman he ever met. On his advice Linnaeus tried to get an interview with the aged Hermann Boerhaave, the most famous doctor of his time. After a week Boerhaave received him at his country estate in the suburbs of Leyden.

Gronovius was helpful to Linnaeus in another way: to him is due the credit of having recognized the importance, the epoch-making character, of *Systema naturae* [System of

Nature], which Linnaeus showed him in manuscript. Gronovius, who came from a wealthy family of scholars and held the office of senator in the city of Leyden, undertook to pay for the printing of the work. Isaak Lawson, a Scottish student who had seen the manuscript in Gronovius's house, also contributed to the printing costs. The manuscript, expanded in a few places, was given to the printer on June 30 and appeared at the end of the year in Latin on eleven pages in giant folio.

Although Linnaeus was urgently advised by Boerhaave to remain longer in Holland, his financial resources were exhausted, and he returned to Amsterdam intending to take a ship home. Before doing so, however, he paid another call on Johannes Burmann; he now wished to see Burmann's herbarium. This meeting, which Linnaeus treats very briefly in his notes, is described in greater detail in reports of the students to whom Linnaeus talked in later years about his youthful memories. According to these accounts Boerhaave himself urged Linnaeus not to fail to pay another call on his student Burmann and informed Burmann of his coming. This time, in striking contrast to the formality of the first visit, Linnaeus was received very cordially and courteously. Burmann was struck by his guest's unusual knowledge and saw with astonishment how Linnaeus could without any particular difficulty identify plants that had been put aside in the herbarium as unknown. Burmann had no trouble in persuading Linnaeus to stay on in Amsterdam and to move into his house as a guest. Linnaeus did not enjoy this hospitality for very long, but in all likelihood it was during this period that he was able to give the manuscript of *Bibliotheca botanica* to the printer Schouten.

In August 1735, on the recommendation of Gronovius and Boerhaave, he was made superintendent of the botanical and zoological garden in Hartekamp belonging to a wealthy banker and patron of culture, George Clifford. Linnaeus spent two happy years, from September 1735 to October 1737, at this country place between Haarlem and Leyden. He reported that here he was treated "like a prince." They "loved him like a son of the house," he "had everything that he could wish for, lodgings than which none more magnificent could be imagined, splendid gardens and greenhouses, a complete botanical library." In addition to this splendid hospitality, Clifford put at Linnaeus's disposal sufficient funds to enlarge the botanical garden with new plants and to procure for the library those books which Linnaeus needed for his work. In the foreword to *Hortus Cliffortianus* [The Clifford Garden], the splendid catalogue that appeared in 1738, Linnaeus gives a vivid description of Hartekamp, together with his first impressions of it:

> My eyes were instantly overwhelmed by so many masterpieces of nature enhanced by artificial means, avenues, flowerbeds, statues, lakes and hills and mazes. I was enchanted with the menagerie filled with tigers, apes, wild dogs, Indian deer and goats, South American and African boars; their voices blended with those of flocks of birds. ... I was astounded when I entered the greenhouses which contained such a wealth of plants that a son of the north could only stand as though bewitched, unable to say to what strange quarter of the earth he had been transplanted.

Here in Hartekamp it became evident that Linnaeus could work with a true frenzy. His huge scientific output could only have been produced by a man who labored as though each day were his last. During the time of his stay in Hartekamp his *Systema naturae, Fundamenta botanica* [Fundamentals of Botany], and *Bibliotheca botanica* were printed. He completed *Genera plantarum* and *Flora Lapponica* [Flora of Lapland] and wrote *Hortus Cliffortianus, Critica botanica*, and some shorter pieces. He also completed and gave to the printer the manuscript on ichthyology left unfinished by his friend Peter Artedi, who was drowned at Amsterdam in 1735.

In the summer of 1736 Linnaeus took a trip to England for which Clifford supplied the funds. He visited the botanical gardens in Chelsea and Oxford and procured plants that were lacking in Hartekamp. As he did everywhere, Linnaeus set out eagerly to become acquainted with famous scholars. In Oxford he met the German-born professor of botany, Johann Jakob Dillenius, who at first hardly treated him like a colleague, since he felt that the first part of *Genera plantarum* was an attack on his own teaching. After meeting Linnaeus, however, Dillenius was convinced of the merits of the sexual system and later became one of his strongest supporters. In London Linnaeus visited the venerable president of the Royal Society, Sir Hans Sloane, to whom Boerhaave had given him a generous letter of recommendation. Through Gronovius and Lawson, Sloane already had a copy of *Systema naturae.*

During his stay at Hartekamp, Linnaeus kept up correspondence with his learned friends. He had now accustomed himself to his new manner of life. "He lived in all the comfort that a mortal could wish; he traveled to Leyden to hear Boerhaave; he drove in a coach and four along the streets of Amsterdam; he could go to Amsterdam whenever he chose or could linger in the beautiful gardens at Hartekamp entirely according to his whim; he was served by a cook and servants and could receive guests at any time in magnificent circumstances." The German painter of plants Georg Dionysius Ehret visited Linnaeus in Hartekamp and worked for him. (Ehret produced the colored copperplate engravings that today adorn the walls of the bedroom at the Linnaeus Memorial in Hammarby near Uppsala.)

How completely this whole period was devoted to work is shown in a single sentence of Linnaeus's autobiography: "I was always solitary, was constantly engaged in thought even when asleep." So green a thumb he had that he was even able to bring a banana plant to bloom, something no one had ever before succeeded in doing in Europe. It was regarded as a marvel.

In October 1737 Linnaeus, surely with no light heart, bade farewell to Hartekamp. He spent the winter in Leyden and there moved on terms of equality in the professorial circles of one of Europe's most renowned universities. He had a particularly close relationship with van Royen, whom he helped in the rearrangement of the Botanical Garden.

Gronovius, too, had Linnaeus's help in the preparation of his *Flora Virginica*, in which he made use of the new principles of classification devised by Linnaeus. A scientific circle in Leyden, to which Linnaeus, Gronovius, Lawson, Gerhard van Swieten, Johann Nathaneal Lieberkühn, and Johann Bartsch belonged, held regular evening meetings; the host would deliver a lecture or give a demonstration, which the other members would then discuss.

Early in 1738 Linnaeus could no longer postpone going home to Sweden. The three-year period of absence had already been exceeded, and his betrothed in Falun was no longer formally bound by her pledge. But shortly before the time planned for his departure he fell ill of a fever, a sort of "cholera," and was given medical treatment by van Swieten. At Clifford's invitation he spent a number of weeks convalescing in his beloved Hartekamp, but his health remained impaired.

Before Linnaeus left Leyden he called on the venerable Hermann Boerhaave to say good-by. He came to the bedside of a gravely ill man. The description of this scene in Linnaeus's writings gives a strong impression that the man who was saying farewell wished to take with him much of the glamour of the greatest of doctors.

Before Linnaeus said good-by to Leyden the ailing Boerhaave had already been so seriously affected by *hydrops thoracis*, which was followed by severe asthma, that he could no longer lie in bed but had to sit up; he had also long since forbidden admittance to anyone. Indeed Linnaeus was the only one allowed in the room to kiss his great teacher's hand with a sorrowful *vale!* Whereupon the feeble old man still had enough strength to raise Linnaeus's hand to his lips and kiss it in turn, saying: "I have lived out my time and my years, have also accomplished what I was allowed, was able, to do. God preserve you, before whom all this still lies ahead. What the world demanded of me it has received; but from you it demands much more. Farewell, my dear Linnaeus!" Tears would permit no more and

when Linnaeus returned to his lodging he received from
Boerhaave a magnificent copy of his *Chemistry.*[2]

With a letter of introduction from van Royen to the botanist and physician Antoine de Jussieu in Paris, Linnaeus now
traveled to that city. On the trip through Brabant the change
in climate refreshed him markedly and he felt "as though
renewed from hour to hour." But he was keenly aware that
he had left blossoming Holland behind him.

As soon as he arrived in Brabant he saw that he had been
transported from a beautiful garden to a meager pasture
where the people were impoverished and the houses miserable. The city of Antwerp had old and magnificent
houses but for the most part needy inhabitants. In Brussels
he saw the beautiful fountains in the squares, the magnificent arsenal, the emperor's sister who was living there,
and the papist religious ceremonies at their most elabo-
rate. He often surveyed this whole fair city from a vantage
point on a wall on its western side. To the east the French
element had already penetrated. Outside of Mons there
was a rigorous inspection since no one with more than 50
livres was allowed to enter; however Linnaeus got
through with some 100 ducats. This town, though not
large, had eleven apothecaries. In the surrounding country coal was mined and slate quarried. At Valenciennes
Linnaeus's trunk was sealed because it contained a quantity of books; for he had brought with him a copy of every
book that he had had printed in Holland.[3]

His short stay in Paris was devoted to a great many calls.
Instead of Antoine de Jussieu, whose time was completely
taken up by his medical practice, his younger brother Bernard, the demonstrator of plants at the Jardin des Plantes,
entertained Linnaeus. Under his guidance Linnaeus could
study the extensive contents of this garden, the collections of
botanical books and the herbaria of both Jussieu brothers, as
well as the famous herbarium made by Tournefort. Bernard

Jussieu also took Linnaeus to his country place in Fontaine-bleau and together they made expeditions to study the riches of the plant kingdom within a wide radius of the French capital. Linnaeus promptly met all the scholars in Paris who were engaged in the natural sciences. Through the good offices of the surgeon and botanist Antoine du Fay, president of the Academy of Sciences, whom Linnaeus had asked for permission to attend one of the sessions of the Academy, he was appointed a corresponding member of that celebrated body. Indeed Linnaeus reported that he was urged to take French citizenship and accept employment in the Academy, but even so tempting an offer could not allay his homesickness.

While in Paris he was a guest in Jussieu's home. There were obviously language difficulties, for it is just at this point in his autobiography that Linnaeus mentions his lack of linguistic talent. In extenuation he points out that time spent abroad is too precious in his eyes for any of it to be squandered in language studies. However he did think it remarkable that he had learned neither English, French, nor German, that he had not learned the language of the Laplanders, and especially that he had not even learned Dutch while living in Holland for three years. "Nonetheless he got along everywhere well and happily." This may well have been true, because he was associating principally with his equals. He emphatically points out that he had refused to adopt French customs. From Paris he traveled to Rouen and from there by sailing ship to his homeland.

4

Medical Practice in Stockholm

Linnaeus landed at Hälsing-
borg and went first to Stenbrohult to see his father, then to
Falun where his engagement with Sara Elisabeth Moraea
was solemnly ratified. His fiancée had had to wait almost four
years for him to redeem his pledge, and now the marriage
was to take place as soon as possible.

Hoping to earn quickly the means with which to establish
a household, Linnaeus betook himself to Stockholm to practice medicine. In the capital he could count on a readier
recognition of the scientific reputation he had gained abroad
than anywhere else. It is questionable, however, that he seriously intended to practice in Stockholm to the end of his
days, as he writes in his reminiscences. He must have been
too well aware of his longing for fame to bury prematurely
all other plans. His secret wishes are revealed in a letter
dated September 15, 1739, to the Swiss scientist Albrecht
von Haller, with whom he had been corresponding since
1737. "Should I come to Uppsala I will completely renounce
medical pratice and devote myself exclusively to plants."[1]
The period in Stockholm would have been only an interlude,
except that he made personal connections of great importance for his future and gained an experience of general

practice that was significant for his later career. "Stockholm received Linnaeus in the month of September 1738 like an outsider. He had the intention of earning his living there as a physician. Since, however, he was unknown to everyone at that time, there was no one who would entrust his precious life to the hands of an untried doctor nor indeed even that of his dog. . . ."[2]

The situation in the Swedish capital at the time was the same as in other cities of Europe. Generally speaking, a doctor could not make a living from independent medical practice; only a post as a court physician or as a municipal or provincial doctor could insure his livelihood, especially since there was competition in the city from barber-surgeons and quacks of all kinds. In a sense, therefore, Linnaeus was exceptional in that he succeeded, after a relatively short period of patient waiting, in becoming a much-sought-after doctor. He seems to have managed this very adroitly.

> When he saw no way to acquire a medical practice, he began to frequent the popular restaurants where young cavaliers who had been wounded *in castris Veneris* [in the service of Venus] sat about. He encouraged them to be of good cheer, to have a glass of Rhine wine, and gave assurance that he would cure them in two weeks. When finally two who had hitherto been treated unsuccessfully placed their lives in his hands and were promptly cured, he had within one month most of the young people under his care. Through this his credit began to rise so that by early March he had a most respectable practice due to the prevailing pox and fevers.[3]

This form of specialization soon proved very profitable, and Linnaeus tried to give his patients the best treatment and the advantages of the latest discoveries. His experience in Holland stood him in good stead here, and so did the advice he got by letter from friends and colleagues abroad. Among other friends, he asked the French physician François Boissier Sauvages de Lacroux for help:

During all of the brief period I spent in Paris I was depend-
ent on my empty purse. Poor was I born and poor have I
always been. Returning to my native land, the star of good
fortune rose for me at the beginning of last year. For some
reason unknown to me, large numbers of patients
streamed my way. I have acquired here in Stockholm, the
capital where I live, a substantial medical practice, perhaps the largest of all the doctors in the country. But, alas,
almost all the young men in our fatherland, as a result of
associating with loose and shameless women, have been
miserably infected with gonorrhea. In Holland I fought
this disease hundreds of times. But now I can hardly go on.
I have heard that you in Montpelier are very experienced
in the treatment of this ailment. In the name of the deep
friendship you have for me I beg you to teach me how it
is cured. I do not need any general theory but prescriptions and a real therapeutic method. Do that and you will
be giving me a thousand ducats a year.[4]

Early in 1739 he reported proudly in a letter[5] that during
the last winter he had had forty to sixty patients under his
care every day. During these months Linnaeus established
an acquaintance with the nobleman Carl Gustaf Tessin, who
as leader of the "Hats" party had great political power.
Thenceforth the upper classes, the nobility, and members of
Parliament sought medical treatment from Linnaeus. Since
these were chiefly Tessin's friends and members of his party,
Linnaeus was jokingly referred to as "Physician in Ordinary
to the Hats." Tessin also put a suite in his house at Linnaeus's
disposal and later on proved the most powerful supporter of
the young doctor, of whose achievements in the realm of
botany, so celebrated abroad, he was also aware.

Through Tessin, Vice-Admiral Theodor Ankarcrona, com-
mander of the Swedish fleet stationed in Stockholm, heard
about Linnaeus and appointed him medical officer to the
admiralty for the Stockholm naval base. On May 15, 1739,
Linnaeus received the official certificate of appointment,
which assured him of a yearly salary of 200 silver talers. The

position of naval doctor was especially attractive to him because it included the care of the sick in the naval hospital.
This hospital consisted of numerous rather small wooden
structures which had been put up in 1737–1738 to replace
barracks built in the seventeenth century. On the average,
between 100 and 200 sick were confined here, among them
quite a number of suffering from the "French evil" [syphilis]
who were kept apart in special rooms. On the hospital staff
the most important man under the chief medical officer was
the chief assistant medical officer to the admiralty, Georg
Heinrich Kranert. Kranert, a barber-surgeon from Lüne-
burg, had been in charge of services in the admiralty hospital
since 1725 and had an unusually good education, not only in
the field of surgery but also in obstetrics. For twelve years he
had looked after the hospital alone, and this practical experience made him in many respects the equal of the new admiralty medical officer. This is obvious from the many reports
written jointly with Linnaeus and addressed to higher naval
authorities, and from the fact that Kranert received the same
yearly salary as Linnaeus and, in recognition of his long service as assistant medical officer to the fleet, an additional
personal allowance of 150 talers. Thus it is not surprising that
Linnaeus, who at first had been zealous about the medical
welfare of the personnel at the station, came to leave this
concern more and more to the capable Kranert.

Another influential member of Tessin's circle was Martin
Triewald, famous for his part in the development of mining
and industrial techniques in Sweden. Since 1728 he had been
giving public lectures on physics and mechanics in the
Knights' Hall in Stockholm. Triewald, himself a member of
the Society of Sciences in Uppsala and also of the Royal Society in London, was engaged at this time with the idea of
founding a Swedish academy of sciences in Stockholm. He
was able to enlist Linnaeus's enthusiasm for his project and
to win over other famous persons. In May 1739 the academy
was founded and Linnaeus elected its first president. At
about the same time he was commissioned to give public
lectures in botany and mineralogy in the Knights' Hall. For
this too, again through the good offices of Marshal Tessin, he

was assured of a fixed remuneration. This lectureship, like that of Triewald on physics and mechanics, was under the supervision of the Mining Council, the highest mining authority in Sweden.

Linnaeus's great pride in what he had accomplished in his first year in Stockholm at the age of thirty-two, is evident in this sentence from his autobiography: "Within a single month Linnaeus becomes public lecturer at the Knights' Hall with a stipend, physican to the admiralty with a salary and first president of the Academy. . . ." Now there was nothing to stand in the way of his marriage. On June 26, 1739, the ceremony was performed at Sweden Farm, the home of his parents-in-law, near Falun. A few months later he returned with his young wife to Stockholm and moved into a small residence called Steward's House.

On May 5, 1741, Linnaeus was called to Uppsala to become Lars Roberg's successor as professor of theoretical and practical medicine. Parliament had just previously commissioned him to undertake a journey to the islands of Öland and Gotland and he began this trip on May 15, therewith ending his medical practice in Stockholm.

5

Uppsala, 1741–1778

After Rudbeck's death in 1740,
Rosén, Linnaeus, and the physician and chemist Johann
Gottschalk Wallerius had been proposed to fill his chair. That
Rosén, who over the years had earned a great reputation for
instruction in medicine, should receive the appointment was
certainly justifiable. But it was not an entirely satisfactory
solution, since Rosén, the experienced clinician, was given at
the same time the chair of theoretical medicine, which also
included instruction in botany and supervision of the Botanical Garden. Linnaeus resented this and expressed his chagrin
in letters to his friends. He wrote to Sauvages on September
20, 1740: "Dr. Nils Rosén, who cannot even recognize a
nettle, has received Rudbeck's post. That's the way things
are going here."[1] But the relationship between Rosén and
Linnaeus was never as dramatic as an early biographer, Dietrich Heinrich Stoever, represented it in his two-volume life
of Linnaeus, published in 1792. It was typical of Linnaeus's
fiery temperament that he met every real or fancied setback
with a sharp rejoinder.

Not long afterward, Lars Roberg, who had occupied the
chair of practical and theoretical medicine for more than
thirty years, resigned for reasons of age. The filling of his

chair created a controversy; in fact it became a scandal not confined to university circles. Rosén, who meantime had become dean of the medical faculty, certainly did not behave with complete propriety. For instance, a demand was made that Linnaeus should prove his knowledge of Latin in a formal, public disputation, but since Linnaeus had written a series of works in Latin, these were considered sufficient proof of his ability.

A much greater uproar was caused by the behavior of Wallerius. He wrote a polemic against Linnaeus entitled *Decades binae thesium medicarum* [Twice Ten Medical Theses] and he defended this work in a public disputation, at which Rosén presided. The students present broke into noisy support of Linnaeus. Some climbed onto chairs, stamped, shouted, and strewed the floor with fragments of the torn thesis. The incident was the subject of parliamentary discussion and censure in Stockholm. Finally influential persons took up Linnaeus's cause, and after the king signed the certificate of appointment on May 5, 1741, all criticism ceased.

On October 27, after a journey of three and a half months through Öland and Gotland and a brief stay in Stockholm, Linnaeus delivered his inaugural lecture, in which he explained the extent to which journeys of research through the provinces of Sweden could be of use to medicine as well. Though at the end of his discourse he made grateful reference to his predecessor and pledged loyalty to the king and to the university chancellor Worte, he was merely observing customary academic courtesy. An obvious reference to the difficulties that had stood in the way of his appointment was his comment that for the majority of the students his coming had been eagerly awaited.

In the great auditorium of the Gustavianum he began on November 3 his announced course of lectures on *Systema morborum* [The Classification of Diseases]. On the same day Rosén and Linnaeus asked the university chancellor for permission to exchange their subjects of instruction. In January 1742 the chancellor granted this request. Rosén now was in charge of the college hospital and was expected to deliver the lectures on anatomy, physiology, etiology, and *Chymia pharmaceutica* [pharamceutical chemistry]. For his part Linnaeus took over the Botanical Garden and the instruction in botany, symptomology, dietetics, materia medica, and natural science in general. From now on Linnaeus was purely a college professor. He gave up general medical practice, treating only friends and on occasion the poor. Nor did he weep for his practice in Stockholm. "By the grace of God I am now freed from the miserable drudgery of that practice in Stockholm; I now hold the position that I have long hoped for. . . ."[2]

That botany continued to be his greatest interest is clearly shown by the zeal with which he enlarged and rearranged the Botanical Garden. In January 1742 he applied to the university senate for funds to build an orangery so that he could raise plants from foreign lands with protection from the unfavorable climate. The money was granted and construction of the two-wing building began. A year later it was ready. He now sought in all quarters for plants and seeds by exchange or as gifts to increase the contents of the garden.

On the grounds of the Botanical Garden, whose beginnings date back to Olof Rudbeck the elder, stood the residence for the garden director, built in 1693. It had gradually fallen into such disrepair that by 1731 the younger Rudbeck could no longer live there. Since this architecturally interesting building contained a valuable library and natural-history collection, it had been extensively fireproofed. Iron doors, window frames, and roof trusses had been installed instead of the usual wooden construction. And so the house had survived the great fire of 1702, which burned large sections of the city to the ground. This house, which Linnaeus described in a letter as being "more like an owl's nest or a robbers' den than a professor's house," was now completely restored. From the first days of his stay at Uppsala until his death, Linnaeus lived in it. It now houses the Linnaeus Museum, having again been restored to approximately its original condition.

In the spring of 1742 Lars Roberg died. From then on Linnaeus received the full salary of a professor. Now he could declare with satisfaction that he lacked for nothing. He had an honorable position at the university, sufficient money, a happy family, and a fine house. He does mention in his autobiography, however, that a substantial part of his fortune had been brought to him by his wife on his marriage.

How widely Linnaeus was recognized abroad as a botanist is evident from the generous support he received for the Botanical Garden. Almost all the important botanists of the time, as well as many lesser-known amateurs, helped by sending seeds of rare plants, an assistance that Linnaeus gratefully acknowledged. Other signs of esteem came from abroad. In January 1743 he was named a member of the Academy of Sciences in Montpellier. This however was not his first membership in a foreign scientific society. During his stay in Holland he had been made a member of the Imperial Leopoldina-Carolina Academy of Naturalists (1736). After the death of his intimate friend Anders Celsius, Linnaeus was made secretary of the Royal Society of Sciences in Uppsala in October 1744 and a little later supervisor of the students' association in the province of Småland. Both these positions had been held by Anders Celsius.

In 1745 Linnaeus opened in the orangery building a museum of natural science (Museum Rerum Naturalium). Its basic inventory consisted of a number of stuffed animals, donated by the university chancellor Count Gyllenborg, and a collection of eighty bottles of preserved amphibians, fishes, and worms, given to Linnaeus by the crown prince elect, Adolphus Frederick of Schleswig-Holstein-Gottorp, after he visited Uppsala, in 1744. In 1745 also Linnaeus's *Flora Suecia* [Flora of Sweden] and *Fauna Suecia* [Fauna of Sweden], were published, as well as his report about his journey to Gotland and Öland.

In 1746 Linnaeus, again with the assistance of Parliament, embarked on an exploratory journey through another Swedish province. This time it was Västergötland, and once more he not only made natural-history observations but carefully recorded everything that was of medical or economic interest.

Linnaeus also seized every opportunity to advance the

natural sciences beyond the boundaries of his own country. For example, he tried to use Sweden's foreign trade relations to arrange voyages abroad for his students. In 1747, at the instigation of Count Tessin, the Swedish East India Company, when its privileges had been renewed, was obliged to provide one student of natural science each year with a free trip to China and back. For such trips, naturally enough, only Linnaeus's students were considered. This marked the beginning of an exodus of many young Swedes on journeys of scientific exploration. These students, whom Linnaeus in his arrogant fashion called his "apostles," not only enriched his collections at home but spread their teacher's fame throughout the world.

In the following year Parliament passed a decree proposed by some members belonging to the circle of Linnaeus's friends that the natural sciences were to be taught in all Swedish schools as a separate subject and that all teachers of the subject were to take an examination. In acknowledgment of the services Linnaeus had rendered by his journey through Västergötland and in recognition of the economic benefits his observations had produced, the king named him, shortly after the printed account of his trip appeared, as Physician in Ordinary (Archiater). This title, however, is to be understood as merely honorific. Linnaeus was never really physician to the king, for that privilege belonged to his faculty colleague Rosén. In later years, when Rosén was occasionally very busy with his duties as Physician in Ordinary in the capital, Linnaeus often spoke out in anger, for at such times the whole burden of faculty responsibility as well as medical instruction fell on him.

With the collections growing larger and larger as a result of donations from friends and from students traveling abroad, the herbaria now were richer in content than the finest that he could remember seeing anywhere. Consequently instruction in botany became so popular that more and more students, as well as many guest auditors from Stockholm and the continent, came to Uppsala. Especially attractive were the large excursions conducted in summertime in the neighborhood of Uppsala.

For every summer when we went botanizing he had a couple of hundred auditors who collected plants and insects, made observations, shot birds, kept records. And after they had botanized from seven in the morning until nine in the evening they came back into the city with flowers in their hats and accompanied their leader with drums and hunting horns through the whole city to the Botanical Garden.[3]

As a textbook for his students Linnaeus put together a catalogue of plants growing in the Botanical Garden under the title *Hortus Upsaliensis* [The Garden of Uppsala]. The work appeared in 1748, the same year in which he published the sixth edition of *Systema naturae*. And yet the other branches of his teaching responsibility did not suffer from his preference for botany. As early as 1742–1743 he gave lectures on dietetics; six years later he gave the course again and taught it for eight semesters altogether, the last time in 1771–1772. This course enjoyed especial popularity with students in other departments as well; he himself reports that up to 300 students attended. It was this particular course that gave Linnaeus the opportunity to influence large numbers of people and to contribute to an improvement of health in general. The substance of these lectures, preserved in notes by students from various departments, indicates that what Linnaeus talked about under the heading of dietetics corresponds in general to what the doctors of antiquity understood by that term. Today such a course would be described as "Principles of Hygiene." His course on drugs, on the other hand, was designed simply for medical students. As textbook for this he published his *Materia medica* in 1749.

On April 29, 1749, Linnaeus embarked, once more at the direction of Parliament, on a journey to the interior. It took him to Skåne, the southernmost province. On his way back he was drawn once more to Stenbrohult, where in the interim his father had died and his only brother, Samuel Linnaeus, had succeeded to the parish.

Linnaeus's important influence on Swedish intellectual life

was aided by the personal relations he was able to establish with the reigning family. The Prince Bishop of Lübeck, Adolphus Frederick of Schleswig-Holstein-Gottorp, had been elected in 1745 as successor to the Swedish throne since the marriage of Frederick I with Ulrica Eleanora had remained childless. In 1744, when Adolphus Frederick visited the University of Uppsala for the first time, the professors were presented to him. On introducing Linnaeus and Anders Celsius, the chancellor of the university emphasized that both men were well known far beyond the boundaries of Sweden. In that same year Adolphus Frederick married Princess Louisa Ulrica of Prussia, sister of Frederick the Great. In charge of the delegation under whose protection the princess traveled from Berlin to Sweden was Linnaeus's friend Carl Gustaf Tessin, who was later appointed lord marshal at the Court. In 1751 Tessin became tutor to Crown Prince Gustaf and when Adolphus Frederick and Louisa Ulrica succeeded to the throne that year he was also appointed the queen's lord chamberlain. In the years 1738 to 1752 Tessin was without question the most powerful man in the Swedish kingdom. Later he lost all political power, in particular the favor of the reigning pair, but as long as he had influence at court, Linnaeus's own relations with the king and queen were good. Louisa Ulrica, who was quite noticeably superior in intellect to her husband, contributed considerably to the business of government, but she also suffered several serious setbacks and finally had to witness the loss of much of the Crown's influence. While her husband is considered insignificant in the line of Swedish monarchs, Louisa Ulrica holds an honorable position in Swedish history as patroness of art, science, and literature. Her interests and activities coincided with those of the art-loving Tessin.

Adolphus Frederick and his queen were both open to the tendencies of their times, partly because of their close connection with the ruling houses on the continent, where the interest in the natural sciences was growing greater and greater. The castles there had their collections of animals and natural curiosities, and the Swedish royal house wished to acquire a collection also. There are plenty of examples in this period of reigning princes acquiring ready-made collections of natural-history specimens for great sums of money. The Amsterdam apothecary Albert Seba, on whom Linnaeus had paid a call, sold his collection to Peter the Great of Russia for 15,000 guilders.

Adolphus Frederick too acquired a noteworthy collection which probably also came from Holland. His gift to the university of animals preserved in alcohol has already been mentioned; presumably these were only his duplicates, since he still had a respectable collection which was housed in Ulriksdal Castle. Louisa Ulrica, originally interested in literature and in collecting coins, medallions, and engravings, became excited by her husband's collections and turned to natural-history specimens too. When Drottningholm Castle was being rebuilt she had brought there the finest specimens from Ulriksdal, especially those that were attractive in appearance. In the assembling of princely natural-history collections, the wish to make a show played a large part in the selection and arrangement. The complete royal natural-history collection was brought to Drottningholm in 1773 when the rooms in Ulriksdal Castle were needed for other purposes; after the accession of Gustavus III in 1771, it had ceased to arouse much interest.

The natural-history objects presented to the University of Uppsala by Adolphus Frederick in 1744 were described by Linnaeus in a dissertation of 1746 entitled *Museum Adolpho-Friderici* [The Adolphus-Frederick Museum]. The king's own collection in Ulriksdal Castle was catalogued by Linnaeus in 1754; however, in the work entitled *Museum Regis Adolphi Friderici* [King Adolphus Frederick's Museum] only the rarer animals are mentioned. He described the collection as "a flawless and splendid cabinet of various animals preserved in alcohol, an immense collection of stuffed birds, an incredible quantity of insects mounted on needles, and shells in cases." The natural-history collection in Drottningholm Castle was arranged by Linnaeus according to his system in 1751, and again in 1752. "Her Majesty the Queen is beginning to take pleasure in the natural sciences and is obtaining from India the most splendid collection of shells and insects, comparable with the greatest in the world." Since the collection consisted principally of shells, he had to study this field, in which "no one had previously made a proper start; so that he had to busy himself with something that he had never thought about before. In this he had the pleasure of daily conversation with such a great and magnificent queen as well as with such a kind king."[4]

From July until September 1751 and during August 1752 Linnaeus lived in Drottningholm Castle and worked exclusively on the mounting and cataloguing of the collections. Louisa Ulrica tells about it in a letter to her mother [written in French]:

> I entertain myself by arranging it [the collection of butterflies and insects] with a professor from Uppsala who is a very great expert and a doctor. He is a most amusing man, possessed of all the wit in the world without the appearance of having it and who entertains me hugely for both these reasons. In the evening he is obliged to walk with the King, and no day passes but that he finds the means of putting everyone in a good humor.[5]

In the middle of December 1752 Linnaeus went to stay in Ulriksdal Castle at the king's command, in order to arrange that collection also, within a period of six weeks. He went to work with his usual fiery zeal. In a letter to his good friend the Swedish physician Abraham Bäck, he wrote: "I have been writing day and night on the description of His Majesty's natural science collection and my eyes are burning and I can hardly close them."[6] This catalogue of the king's collection, the second part of which appeared in 1764, was the result of three visits to Ulriksdal Castle, lasting nine weeks in all. It took Linnaeus a total of thirteen weeks to make the description of the collection in Drottningholm Castle which appeared in 1764 under the title *Museum Ludovicae Ulricae Reginae* [The Museum of Queen Louisa Ulrica] and comprised 720 printed pages.

Today anyone who is interested in how the princely natural-science collections of the eighteenth century were assembled will be amazed to discover that the prices paid were often out of all proportion to the worth of the objects; this was true of those at Ulriksdal and Drottningholm. The collections were acquired abroad, usually complete, though valuable or supposedly valuable individual items were often bought separately. Anatomical preparations were also much sought after. At Ulriksdal there were human embryos. Even a fetus miscarriage of Queen Louisa Ulrica was included, and an elephant embryo that had been bought from Seba in Amsterdam. These embryos were concealed behind a silk curtain so that the queen and other female visitors would not sustain a shock during pregnancy. Since the payments for these natural-history collections usually came from a ruler's privy purse there is no way now to estimate even approximately the actual expenditures.

Close contact with the royal couple, in conformity with the custom of the time, was of great value to Linnaeus and to his students as well. In 1754 at his request the queen redeemed for the sum of 14,000 copper talers the great collections made by Linnaeus's student Friedrick Hasselquist in Egypt and Palestine, which had been attached by the government in Turkey after Hasselquist's death.[7] Earlier she had acquired the greater part of the collection of insects and plants brought from North America by Linnaeus's student Pehr Kalm. Linnaeus arranged a mineral collection for Count Tessin, who had also become interested in the natural sciences.

> Count Tessin was also fascinated by this science, especially by rocks and snails, and the countess loved botany. And so Linnaeus had raised his science from nothingness in Sweden to the highest peak, since it was loved and fostered by important and even royal personages. Such is the result of diligence![8]

A special token of royal grace and recognition was the bestowal on Linnaeus of the Knight's Cross of the Order of the Polar Star, "a favor which in Sweden had never before been awarded to a doctor, a physician in ordinary, or a

professor." And then, in 1762, Linnaeus was actually ele-
vated to the nobility, and that retroactively to 1757. The coat
of arms assigned to him, for which he had been allowed to
submit sketches, shows as crest and as outer border of the
mantle the shoots and flowers of his favorite plant, which at
Gronovius's suggestion had been renamed *Linnaea borealis.*
Linnaeus loved this flower so much that he would allow no
portrait of himself to be painted without a branch of it. The
Linnaeus Museum in Uppsala contains a Chinese tea service
decorated with *Linnaea* motifs, which Linnaeus had made
on special order, with the help of the East India Company.

In the years 1747, 1759, and 1772 Linnaeus served as rector of the university. But far more important were his activities within the medical department. In a letter to the Austrian botanist Nikolaus Joseph von Jacquin he describes his
usual daily schedule:

Every day I give a one-hour public lecture, then I hold a
kind of private seminar with a number of students. After
that I spend one hour with Danish students and two with
Russians. And so, having talked for five hours before lunch,
in the afternoon I read proof, write manuscripts for the
printers and letters to my botanical friends, visit the garden and see those who come to visit me; I also look after
my bit of land, and this means that on many days I barely
have time to eat. If you saw me you would certainly pity
my lot, for here am I, surrounded by a large family, and
yet I must make time to visit with both my compatriots
and foreigners arriving here. While my colleagues can
constantly enjoy the amenities of life, I have to work day
and night on the investigation of a science that a thousand
men will not be able to complete, to say nothing of the
time I squander every day on scientific correspondence
and so bring upon myself a premature old age. If the
Almighty grants me a few more years I will release the
aging horse from the yoke so that he will not entirely
collapse and end by being a laughing stock. If then I suc-

ceed in having in my garden a few rare plants I shall rejoice in them.[9]

In 1758 Linnaeus acquired for the sum of 80,000 talers the Hammarby estate situated six miles from Uppsala. In 1762 he enlarged the buildings "when he noticed that he was weak and wished his children to have shelter." He spent his summers in Hammarby and gave private instruction to visitors from abroad. A garden was laid out with foreign plants, many of them from Siberia. On a hill behind the manor he had a small stone structure built for storing his collections. He had decided on this "museum on the hill" after his valuable collections in Uppsala had only barely been rescued from a fire. In 1880 this country estate was acquired by the Swedish government, and today it is a Linnaeus Memorial where many mementos gathered by the Swedish Linnaean Society are exhibited. The main residence has been extensively restored to its state during Linnaeus's lifetime, and whoever seeks a living impression of the great naturalist will find it easy to set back the clock by two centuries and picture him and his family there.

When Linnaeus acquired Hammarby he was the father of an imposing family. Of seven children five had survived. The first child had come into the world in Stockholm in 1741— a son named Carl after his father. Of the four daughters, the youngest, Sophia, was just one year old; the eldest, Elisabeth Christina, was fifteen. The numerous descendants of Linnaeus in Sweden today are all the offspring of these two daughters.

Linnaeus has relatively little to say about his family life. In his autobiographical writings there are only brief notices of the births of his children and of the deaths of a daughter and a son. Nor is there much to be learned from his letters. However, the German naturalist and pioneer technologist Johann Beckmann who became a Göttingen professor, in the diary of his journey through Sweden in 1765–1766 gave a detailed account of Linnaeus at home.[10] Beckmann visited Linnaeus both in Uppsala and in Hammarby. His first meeting with the

"Herr Archiater and Knight Linnaeus" occurred on September 6, 1765.

Because it was vacation time when I arrived in Uppsala the Herr Archiater was at Hammarby, his country place. However, he was expected back in Uppsala that same day, and so in the meantime I went into a bookstore and found there a not tall, somewhat elderly man with dusty shoes and stockings, a long beard, and an old green coat on which hung a medal. I was not a little astonished to be told that this was the famous Linnaeus. When he was preparing to leave I addressed him, speaking in Latin because he does not fully understand German. He immediately recalled my correspondence and was extremely polite. Because he had come in from the country on foot he was sweaty and he hurried to his Uppsala home, taking me with him.

Linnaeus lodged his German guest at his home and was very much interested in his further travel plans. When Beckmann mentioned that he was going to Falun, Linnaeus immediately wrote a letter of introduction to his brother-in-law. About the arrangement of the house Beckmann reports:

In the living room hung his portrait with the *Linnaea* in his hand, as well as portraits of the most famous botanists, and plans of several botanical gardens. We fell to talking about insects, and immediately after he had shown us the collection he had in his house, we went out into the splendid garden, and I cannot describe with what happy excitement he sought out and exhibited the plants which he had not yet seen because they had sprung up since his departure.

In October Beckmann went to see Linnaeus at his country estate in Hammarby.

He received me in the most friendly fashion and urged me to remain for several days which, however, I could not do because of the rented coach. At this estate, to which some nearby farms belong, he has plastered the walls of his rooms with so many copper engravings of plants taken from the rarest books such as Sloane, Ehrets, etc., that they look exactly like wallpaper. Some of these were done in water colors by Herman in the East Indies and later were printed in *Horto Malabarico* [The Garden in Malabar]. Frau Archiater is a daughter of the late mine doctor Moraeus and is not so charming toward strangers as her husband. Her very plain way of dressing does little to improve her appearance. When at dinner Herr Archiater said to her jokingly: "I've brought another German home; you must really learn German so that you can join in the conversation," she replied that it was really not worth while to learn German *för herrens skul* [for the gentleman's sake]. I said in my broken Swedish that she was right, *men jag skall lera Svenska för fruens skul* [but I will learn Swedish for the lady's sake]. This made the Herr Archiater laugh, and she seemed to be somewhat more genial after that. I spent the day most agreeably discussing various matters and found out from him many things that I wanted to know; in the course of it we enjoyed several pipefuls of tobacco. And so I went off that evening, much pleased.

Linnaeus's family feeling was intense, and particularly evident in the way he raised his son to be his successor. His single male heir, destined to go down in history with little fame as Carolus Linnaeus the younger, was forced into the study of natural science very early, and Linnaeus's older pupils were constantly obliged to assist him. Through his father's influence he received honors and distinctions while still a youth, as when, at eighteen (1759), he was appointed demonstrater in botany at the University of Uppsala. In 1763 he was promised by order of the king that he would succeed to his father's chair. Two years later the crown prince, who at this time was Chancellor of the University, ordered the department of medicine at Uppsala to bestow upon him an

M.D. degree. This, together with the earlier appointments, gave rise to envy and distrust, for the young son of the Archiater had no conspicuous gifts or any great amount of knowledge. Linnaeus remarked in his autobiography: "In 1763 Linnaeus was granted exemption from teaching duties and his son was raised to a full professorship because of his father's services, although he was only twenty-one years old. But the father administered the office for him until he was able to do so himself."[11]

6

~~~~~~≫≪~~~~~~

The Final Years

Sickness always played an important role in Linnaeus's life. There is repeated mention of it in his letters and autobiographical writings. In his prime he was frequently plagued by migraine headaches, which could be precipitated by rather minor causes, especially by anger and excitement. For example, he reported in 1756, noting the exact date,[1] how the carelessness of his gardener in the Botanical Garden in Uppsala was enough to cause him a "most severe" attack of migraine. In letters to friends he mentioned repeatedly how much trouble he had with migraine, and he begged his medical correspondents for advice from their own experience with its treatment. His own opinion about it was that scholars and persons leading a sedentary life were often susceptible to it. Later on, when the attacks decreased in frequency, Linnaeus attributed this to his newly acquired habit of drinking fresh spring water in the early morning and taking physical exercise before his midday meal.

Whereas migraine cast a shadow over at least two decades of his life, he was able to overcome a rheumatic inflammation of the joints more quickly. He attributed the alleviation of the pain to his custom of eating great quantities of fresh wild strawberries, as soon as the painful swelling of the joints began in his feet. Fortunately this ailment always occurred at the time of year when fresh strawberries were available. In later years too, he continued his wild-strawberry cure summer after summer and gave it the credit for his improvement in general well-being. In letters to Sauvages[2] he recommended this cure most warmly, but he also pointed out that unfortunately wild strawberries could not be preserved for the winter in such a way as to retain their efficacy. His praise of wild strawberries caused so much interest among sufferers from rheumatism in Uppsala that the price on the market rose rapidly, and he, the initiator of the treatment, had to pay almost ten times the former price. He made only brief mention of a kidney stone which gave him trouble during the year he was working on *Species plantarum*: "While he was writing this book, which he completed in one year, he observed for the first time the formation of a kidney stone, unmistakably due to sitting still and to pressure on the right side of the body in the neighborhood of the kidney."[3]

In May 1764, Linnaeus came down with a feverish illness, which cannot be identified today with any certainty, although prescriptions recommended for him and details of symptoms and diagnosis are contained in his letters and autobiographical writings. He wrote that he was close to death, and the illness must indeed have been serious, for he entrusted himself to treatment by his departmental colleagues Nils Rosén and Samuel Aurivillius. The latter was Rosén's son-in-law and eventual successor to his chair. After almost two months in bed Linnaeus was finally able to overcome this feverish infection, which in all probability was either a paratyphus or a severe case of influenza, and he outlived both the doctors who attended him. Aurivillius died of spotted fever in 1767 at the age of forty-five. Linnaeus's personal relations with Rosén, which in earlier years had been so troubled, grew substantially better after his illness—Linnaeus himself spoke of an "unimaginable friendship." In 1768 Rosén in his turn called on his colleague to take charge when he fell ill of the intermittent fever known as "Uppsala fever." Linnaeus also attended Rosén in his final illness, colic of the kidneys and attacks of asphyxia, which ended in his death on July 16, 1773.

The closer Linnaeus came to his last decade the more frequent were his illnesses and the more marked their effect on his productivity. As early as 1772 he believed that his days were numbered, and the following year he suffered from severe lumbago and sciatica. In 1774 he received the first "message of death" in the form of a stroke. The paralysis, to be sure, lessened, but his system was considerably impaired. Two years later came a second stroke, and this was the last year in which he made auobiographical notes: "Linnaeus limps, and hardly walks, speaks indistinctly, can scarcely write." Visitors still came from abroad and were allowed to see him, but he could barely converse with them. His interest in his surroundings became less and less, and only in the presence of his students, when the conversation turned to things with which he had been occupied all his life, did he appear to rouse himself.

The last summer of his life, that of 1777, was spent in his beloved Hammarby where, when the weather permitted, he would have himself taken into the garden or up to his little museum, the small stone house on the hill where his precious collections were displayed. He would sit there, enjoying the sight of what he had brought together and what he had accomplished, and this experience always enlivened the semiconscious mind of the old man, or so those around him reported. But with autumn came a more rapid decline in his physical and mental forces. Completely helpless and cut off from everything around him, he lived on for a few weeks in Uppsala until in January 1778 death released him.

A solemn funeral took place on January 23. His student Adam Afzelius, who was responsible for the first publication of Linnaeus's autobiography, wrote forty-five years later:

> The burial of Linnaeus in the cathedral at Uppsala was the most solemn occasion I had witnessed up to that time and made such a deep impression on me that I shall never forget it. It was a sad, still evening, the darkness relieved only by the torches, lights, and lanterns of the funeral

cortège moving slowly through the city—the peasants from his property dressed in mourning followed the hearse, carrying lanterns—and the quiet of the evening was disturbed only by subdued murmuring of the crowds of people on the streets and the dull clangor of the majestic main bell.[4]

7

Personality and Image

Some particulars in the account of Linnaeus's public career, particulars that correspond in style and content to his own notes, have already revealed aspects of his essential character. Often he seems like a child of fortune, to whom friends and patrons give help at just the right moment, clearing his path of difficulties that would have brought anyone else to grief. At such times he himself believed that he felt the hand of fate guiding him, and he was perhaps not altogether aware how much his personal ambition and his intellectual abilities determined his career. However, if one wishes to view the course of his life, his influence, and his scientific work as a unified whole, one must take into account not only his relation to his times but his own physical and psychological makeup.

In this regard Linnaean research in recent years has produced much new material, in the form of valuable facts, and supplementary viewpoints. Above all, the works of Elis Malmeström deserve attention, especially those that deal with Linnaeus's attitude toward religion.[1] The recognition that an interrelationship exists between mind and body, even in the career and influence of important men, is a distinguishing mark of the biographical literature of the first half of the twentieth century. Entirely in accord with this point of view is the biography of Linnaeus by Knut Hagberg,[2] in which the material is presented in the Swedish text with the seductive verbal beauty of prose poetry. A study of these recent works in comparison with earlier biographies will show how much has been gained. For the first time Linnaeus becomes more than the great legendary natural-history researcher; he is seen as a human being, and the marble monument to culture turns into flesh and blood.

Linnaeus's physical appearance is known to us through numerous portraits, reports of his own, and descriptions by his contemporaries. Among the portraits the one painted in 1775 by Alexander Roslin, the most important Swedish portrait painter of the time, is pre-eminent—in Linnaeus's opinion as well—because of its excellent likeness and because it shows him in the way he wished to be remembered by future generations. How well the masterly hand of Roslin has captured the true Linnaeus is attested by the literary evidence about his appearance. He himself reported that he was of medium height, rather smaller than average, neither thin nor really fat but somewhat muscular. He had a large head with a pronounced occiput. His hair, light in his youth later became dark, and in his old age gray. His brown eyes, were lively and sharp, with remarkable powers of vision. His brow became wrinkled as he grew old. He had a wart on his right cheek and several on the right side of his nose. His teeth from youth onward were painful and subject to cavities. All who met him were principally impressed by his eyes, which must have had an expression of kindliness; it is there in Roslin's portrait. Count Tessin wrote in his diary: "In his eyes shine all the intelligence and lively fire that must animate a person who ventures into the dark mazes of nature in order to penetrate them and show others the way ahead."[3] Johann Christian Fabricius, an entomologist born in Tondern who was later professor of natural history at the University of Kiel, was with Linnaeus in Uppsala from 1762 to 1764, and he has recorded his impression in these words: "The expression of his face was open, almost always cheery . . . his eyes were the handsomest I have ever seen."[4]

That Linnaeus could endure physical hardship is shown in his report on his trip to Lapland. But whether the robustness of a healthy body or the ambition of a researcher thirsty for knowledge was the determining factor it would be hard to decide. The bodily ills that plagued his earlier years have already been mentioned, and it is entirely consistent with what we hear about his psychic makeup that he suffered for long periods from migraine, an illness that is relatively frequent in just such psychically changeable and highly differentiated persons.

To portray Linnaeus's character is certainly not so easy as some would make it appear. He has often been represented as a man foreordained to greatness, a simplification that cannot satisfy the present-day psychological view of personality. Nor is it sufficient to see him simply as an empiricist, or to emphasize the optimism that was so conspicuous in many phases of his life, or to attempt to explain his unusually highly developed self-assurance simply by his naiveté. Out of the many and various materials, the biographer must construct a more consistent picture of him, take into account the continuity of his personality structure, and investigate the growth in its power of penetration as it matured to the height of his creativity.

In his younger years, especially when he achieved successes, Linnaeus showed a positive attitude toward life, a completely optimistic joy in existence. He could be cheerful and relaxed; he could give exaggerated expression to his feelings, with incomparable richness of fantasy. Even in later life there were always times when he could happily gather students and friends around him in a spirit of merriment and good cheer. "When he noticed that he was weary and dull, he would lay his work aside and seek an evening of good fellowship in which he greatly rejoiced, joking and laughing heartily. With his sanguine temperament he was easily moved to joy, sorrow and anger."[5] According to Fabricius, "His heart stood open to every impulse of joy; he loved jokes, good company, and especially good living. He was a splendid host, charming in company, full of wit and apt anecdotes; but he was also quick to anger, and vehement, though this was over almost instantly.[6] The letter from Queen Louisa Ulrica already quoted mentions Linnaeus's cheerfulness and contagious good humor.

Not surprisingly, the writings he produced in such periods of enhanced well-being embody descriptions that are impressive for their unusual vividness, striking similes, and lively examples. He could, as Malmeström has said, paint with words, and in doing so he showed a preference for strong colors.[7] However, it is important to remember that the language of the eighteenth century cannot be directly compared with that of the present. In those days writers were prone to express themselves vigorously, and one gets the feeling in Linnaeus's case that he took pleasure in especially pregnant word combinations. In his travel reports, particularly in dealing with scenes and circumstances from peasant life that struck him as comic, harsh criticisms are often followed by humorous observations, occasionally with clearly sarcastic overtones. His pleasure in real situation comedy is illustrated, for instance, by his descriptions in a letter to Bäck[8] of the apes that were kept at Drottningholm Castle: he makes special mention of the similarity to human behavior, without however seeing anything more in this than comedy. Johann Beckmann's description of his visit to Linnaeus's house, quoted earlier, also shows his sense of humor.

If as a young man Linnaeus sought out the company of friends and like-minded people, as the trip to Holland abundantly proves, this was not merely an indication of his pleasure in exchanging scientific ideas but proof of his ease in getting along with other people. This also applied to his relations with women, about which, naturally enough, most of the information comes from his earlier years. While he was a student in Uppsala and during his visits to Falun, for example, he was certainly no friend to sorrow. In the home of his benefactor Rudbeck there even seem to have been quarrels because of him. One of Mrs. Rudbeck's female friends, who provided abundant material for the scandalmongers of Uppsala, is said to have shown more partiality for the brown-eyed young student than the mistress of the household approved of. Though the exact circumstances are not known, the fact that Linnaeus left the Rudbeck house abruptly suggests that serious differences must have arisen. There is additional evidence elsewhere that young Linnaeus was a darling of the ladies, and he himself hinted as much several times in his report on his Lapland journey.

Even though his personal friendships were not numerous, some of them were marked by special warmth, among these were his attachment to the friend of his youth, Peter Artedi, and his long association with Bäck. Linnaeus's many letters attest his deep trust in that influential physician in ordinary and president of the medical school. He describes Bäck as "my profoundly honorable, unassuming, and most loyal friend" and repeatedly as my "single true friend in this world."[9]

All his life Linnaeus was extremely sensitive to failure and lack of recognition. There are many examples of this tendency in his correspondence and in his dealings with leading scholars. It is obvious that at times a gloomy pessimism dominated his emotional life. Toward the end of his student days he went through a serious mental-emotional crisis, the result, he thought, of external reverses: his scholarships had not been paid and the problems of livelihood had become acute. Psychically he was completely exhausted and became convinced that a quiet, retired life in the country was better, more worth working for, than the irritations of an academic career. At this same time, too, began the conflict with Rosén, who had already achieved academic success. But the altercation, as Malmeström in particular has pointed out, probably took place chiefly in Linnaeus's mind. Even though he writes in his autobiography that he has sworn to do away with his adversary and with himself, there is no indication that there was ever an open break. In time he weathered this crisis unaided.

During the last three decades of his life, periods of moodiness and genuine depression, nervous restlessness and irritability, fear of death and the wish to retreat from everything severely tried him and those about him. Thus in the year 1748 he was plunged into such a state of despondency that he thought all the world was conspiring against him. A decree of the Royal Chancellery forbidding the printing of books abroad seemed to him directed solely against himself; he declared that its purpose had been to injure him alone and was only with difficulty persuaded that this was not the case. Not even the fact that Count Tessin had been one of the signers of this decree dissuaded him from this compulsive notion. In letters to Bäck he admits his condition: "I confess that for a long time now I have loved quietude and peace; I have no desire to sail forth if I can remain in port. . . ."[10] "Since in my darkness I have nothing to cheer you with I must report the news of others. . . ."[11] These periods of despair occurred again and again, to a point best described in a letter to Bäck in 1758:

> I can write no more, my weary hand fails me. I am a child of misfortune; if I had had a noose and courage, I would have hanged myself long since. I fear my wife is pregnant again; I am old, gray, exhausted, and the room is already full of children; who will feed them? It was an unlucky hour when I accepted this professorship; if I had remained with my golden practice I should be all right now. . . .[12]

He and those around him believed that these states of mind were due to overwork and other external circumstances. Others, Malmeström among them, say that such expressions of temperament are by no means surprising in a Swede, that in fact they represent typical and essential Scandinavian characteristics.[13] However, in many instances Linnaeus's emotional attitudes and behavior are certainly far removed from the normal psychic makeup even of a Scandinavian. In the light of all the evidence, Linnaeus should rather be described as a personality characterized by alternating manic and depressed moods, and with certain schizoid characteristics, which with increasing age became actually pathological. In the last years of his life, the picture of his personality is completely dominated by symptoms of progressive hardening of the arteries of the brain.

Much has been written and speculated about Linnaeus's pre-eminent self-assurance, his vanity, his quest for fame.

These character traits do not fit well with the picture of "the pious and harmonious flower king," the biographer's ideal. The motto on his coat of arms, which he himself selected, is *Famam extendere factis* [To spread reputation through deeds], a clear indication that he sought applause and recognition because it was an inner necessity of his being.

How much Linnaeus helped to advertise the significance and value of his scientific labors is indicated by his own pronouncements; as expressions of self-praise they can hardly be outdone. He describes his book *Species plantarum* as "the greatest in the realm of science," his *Systema naturae* as a "masterpiece that can never be read and admired enough," and *Clavis medicinae* [Key to Medicine] as the "fairest jewel in medicine." In a petition to Parliament he writes of himself: "I have built anew the whole science of natural history from the ground up, to the point where it is today; I do not know whether anyone now can venture forward without being led by my hand." "Many have thought that *Species plantarum* or *Systema naturae* alone would have been enough work for the lifetime of one man."[14] In his autobiographical notes he left the following list of accomplishments:

> No one has practiced his calling with more zeal and more auditors at our university.
>
> No naturalist has undertaken more observations of nature.
>
> No one has had such complete insight into all three kingdoms of nature at once.
>
> No one was a greater botanist or zoologist.
>
> No one has written more orderly or better works, from his own experience.
>
> No one has so completely reformed the whole science and brought it into a new epoch.
>
> No one has had so extensive a correspondence throughout the whole world.
>
> No one has sent out so many students into so many parts of the world.

No one was more famous throughout the world.

No one was a member of more scientific societies. . . .[15]

Though the real purpose of his autobiographical writings may have been to provide material for his academic *Laudatio funebris* [funeral oration], superlatives nevertheless flowed all too easily from his pen. Even in letters to his friends, including Bäck, modesty about his scientific work was nonexistent. He had a habit of writing anonymous reviews of his own books and getting them printed in appropriate places, for example, in the years before his trip to the continent, in the *Hamburgische Berichte.*[16] In his published works he often failed to give credit to other authors; hence much that was actually the work of others was attributed to him. It is hard to decide whether he always did this deliberately, or whether his source references were sparse because he underestimated the work of others and so tended to lose track of their names. Certainly this practice was the cause of many disagreements with other scholars.

That he lent a willing ear to flatterers is not surprising in a man with so marked a need for recognition. In apparent contradiction is the fact that he sometimes showed complete awareness of his vanity and his ambition for fame. This self-knowledge certainly reveals something of a naïve and childish disposition, though it cannot be called a dominant and explanatory character trait. For a tenable explanation of his self-assurance heightened to vanity, it is probably necessary to consider the periods when his spirits sank and his joy in work was dampened to the point of absolute dislike of creativity, when he suffered from grave feelings of inadequacy precisely in the realm of his scientific work and sometimes even threatened to destroy his completed manuscripts. At such times he was totally unproductive and neglected his correspondence as well. This explains why, to the eyes of later generations, these phases of his life are less apparent than those that were filled with an overpowering creative urge. His heightened self-confidence could be represented as an essential characteristic of his nature, although actually it was only an evidence of the exaggerated deflection of his emotional barometer in one direction, as is typical in manic-depressive personalities.

Man's place in nature was redefined by Linnaeus, but his image of the world continued to be that of his time. It was strongly marked by the impression of the parental parsonage, and in his writings and letters he often represented himself as a believing Christian who accepted the subordination of man to God's omnipotence as incontrovertible fact. According to Oscar Levertin, he is "of all the men of the century the only great writer who thinks biblically, feels biblically, and writes biblically."[17] The Psalmist's bipolar form of expression corresponded with his own way of thinking and he was fond of making use of it, as for example in a prose poem which appeared in his description of his journey through Dalecarlia:

> Thou, great Creator and Preserver of all things,
> Thou who didst place us so high in the
>   mountains of Lapland,
> In the mine at Falun—so far in the depths;
> Didst show us day without night in the mountains
>   of Lapland,
> In the mine at Falun night without day
> Praised be all Thou hast made from beginning
>   to end.[18]

He was certain of the constant presence of God; he was grateful to the Creator for having been given, as if he were a "second Adam," the task of arranging nature and assigning names to the members of its three kingdoms—clear evidences of his religious point of view. In no other naturalist of the period does the conviction of being the Lord's elect, predestined of God, find such clear expression. For this reason, he felt sure that none of his colleagues could equal him in science, let alone excel him; to him only this task had been given. The awareness of this mission shows frequently in his notes, and most emphatically in his autobiography:

God himself guided him with his own almighty hand.
He caused him to see more of creation than
   any other mortal before him.
He bestowed on him the greatest insight into natural
   history, greater than any other had ever received.[19]

The privilege of working on a divine assignment became
in his mind the need to work, the mainspring of his zeal, and
this explains much about his attitude toward those who did
not agree with his scientific views. It may also help to explain
his extreme self-confidence.

Although Linnaeus left many other similar indications of
his religious attitude, there are also expressions that are not
understandable or that can only with difficulty be interpreted. Malmeström[20] and other writers have pointed out,
sometimes indirectly, many such open questions or contra-
dictions. A thorough discussion of this subject would be of
great interest, but here there is space only to call attention
to these interrelated elements which are so important in
understanding not only Linnaeus but the whole Swedish intellectual life of the period.

One thing is certain: Linnaeus was by no means a typical
representative of the Enlightenment. This becomes crystal
clear if one tries to draw parallels with Voltaire. However,
the Enlightenment found different historical and intellectual
forms of expression in Sweden than in the rest of Europe. In
Holland Linnaeus came in contact with the ideas of the early
Enlightenment, and Malmeström has drawn attention to his
connection with physico-theology, which attempted to demonstrate through the study of nature the purposeful harmony
of creation, also taking into account the existence of evil.
How concerned Linnaeus was, even at an advanced old age,
with the question of justifying God's ways is proved by his
Nemesis divina [Divine Nemesis]. In any discussion of his
religious attitude, this work requires further examination. If
he regarded his research into nature as a mission in the light
of the physico-theological system of thought, then of necessity over the years, because of his intensive concern, he must

have found more and more discrepancies between his logical conclusions and the Christian belief in God.

That his work as a naturalist and taxonomist shows intuitive characteristics and lacks logical consistency is completely in accord with the fact that he was simply not a thinker in the philosophic sense. At no time did he present his views on life in a clear, understandable form, nor did he always succeed in making the superabundant conclusions of his scientific investigations agree with the fundamental concepts of ecclesiastical belief. From the beginning of his teaching career, the influence of his lectures extended far beyond his own department and Beckmann's travel report contains indications of his troubled relations with the representatives of theology. "When Herr Archiater became professor he gave a course *De generatione hominis* [Concerning the Origin of Man] which displeased the theologians so much that he dared not give it again."[21] This reprimand obviously had a lasting effect on Linnaeus, as did his disagreement with a well-known orthodox theologian, Professor Engelbert Halenius, in the course of an academic disputation in 1748. These events explain the caution of his formulations, which are sometimes incomprehensible. It must be remembered that with his increasing importance among wide circles of the Swedish population his opinions carried more and more weight, and critical distrust on the part of an influential theologian might have serious consequences, not simply for him but for the whole body of his work. His lectures, which were regularly audited by many students of theology, had far-reaching influence; the fact is that presently his ideas and definitions were being heard in sermons throughout the country. A conversation with Beckmann on October 31, 1765, about the souls of animals shows how cautious Linnaeus felt it necessary to be, and his interlocutor considered it so important that he made notes:

> But how these souls think and choose, this is something that will always remain hidden from the naturalist. One must believe what the theologians demand, just as a Catholic, disregarding his own eyes, must consider bread the

body of Christ. Revelation is completely consistent with nature but not in the way the theologians distort it with their explanations. At the outset they knew too little about the natural world, which revelation is intended to complete, and now their self-interest will brook no alteration. At the same time he [Linnaeus] begged me never to dispute with theologians again in this fashion, since they would never change but would only grow to hate natural history, and that could be very harmful to the latter. I must assert, however, that Herr Archiater loves religion and has the most exalted conceptions of God, and certainly his children are brought up in the fear of God. He himself has read the Bible often and with attention, which can be concluded from the aptness of his frequent quotations from Scripture, not only in his writings but in conversation as well.[22]

This is a clear expression of what one can gather, sometimes only in the form of hints, from a study of Linnaeus's notebooks. The key position that he had managed to achieve in this time of tension between faith and knowledge made a decision mandatory, yet he evaded it and chose to compromise. To resolve the conflict with the decisiveness and calm of a philosopher was impossible for him on account of his personality structure as conditioned by his heredity and working environment. The tragic quality of his life—that he could survey and classify the phenomena of nature in their multiplicity better than any of his contemporaries, sometimes with the ebullient zeal of a successful and happy period, and at the same time, well hidden from those on the outside, be concerned to trace the controlling hand of God behind the things of the world and their living appearance —is revealed only by a few indications which are for that reason all the more important. To be sure, Linnaeus was not the only naturalist of his time to be caught in this conflict. In his case, however, we not only meet it in a fashion typical of the Swedish Enlightenment, but one would seek in vain for a picture of his total personality and an understanding of his work without recognizing this element in Linnaeus the man.

The short work *Nemesis divina,* already mentioned, is another valuable source for the interpretation of his view of life. It was not published during his lifetime, but he mentioned it frequently in conversation and in his printed works and letters.[23] The time of its composition cannot be exactly determined, but it is not in any case a work of his old age. Linnaeus gave the manuscript the name of the Greek goddess of vengeance, although it is a collection of examples of punishment meted out by the Old Testament God of vengeance, but it also contains ideas from Swedish folklore and shows, as Ehnmark has pointed out, the influence of contemporary thought.[24] The Old Testament conception of a punishing and avenging deity, which is closely related to the Babylonian-Assyrian principle of an eye for an eye, is illustrated by examples proving that an action that is not, or cannot be, punished by earthly judges will be avenged by God. Accordingly man cannot escape punishment, and evil too is subordinated to the power of God and therefore does not run counter to the system of divine world order. This reflects Leibniz's concept that ultimately it is the will of God that has shaped the whole course of events. Linnaeus's divine nemesis has the force of a moral theodicy; he himself spoke of a *theologia experimentalis* [experimental theology].

It is evident from the manuscript that Linnaeus intended this work for his son, to whom he wished to demonstrate the action of supernatural justice and to emphasize faith in it as a guiding principle for his own life. To this end he used many examples, including the real names of those stricken to increase credibility. The fact that the nemesis is expressed in the manuscript of his *Diaeta naturalis* [Natural Diet] as early as 1733, shows how dominant the thought of divine justice always was for him; later he seems to have viewed it as an underlying factor of dietetics.

The farmhouse at Råshult where Carolus Linnaeus was born

Nils Linnaeus, father of Carolus

Christina Broderson Linnaeus, mother of Carolus

Sketches made by Linnaeus during his Lapland journey in 1732: *(top left)* Observation of the midnight sun; *(bottom left)* A Lapp carrying a boat; *(below)* Owl's head

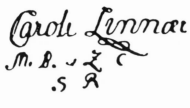

HORTUS UPLAN·DICUS.

Sive

Enumeratio Stirpium, qvæ in variis Hortis uplandicis, imprimis autem in Botanica Publico Upsaliensi coluntur. Methodo propria in clas. ses distributa

Upsal. MDCCXXX

Linnaeus's sketch (1730) for a title page for *Hortus Uplandicus*

CAROLI LINNÆI, *SVECI*,

DOCTORIS MEDICINÆ,

SYSTEMA NATURÆ,

SIVE

REGNA TRIA NATURÆ

SYSTEMATICE PROPOSITA

PER

CLASSES, ORDINES,
GENERA, & SPECIES.

O *JEHOVA! Quam ampla sunt opera Tua !*
Quam ea omnia sapienter fecisti !
Quam plena est terra possessione tua !

Pfalm. civ. 24.

LUGDUNI BATAVORUM,

Apud THEODORUM HAAK, MDCCXXXV.

EX TYPOGRAPHIA

JOANNIS WILHELMI DE GROOT.

Title page of the first edition of *Systema naturae* (Leyden, 1735)

Linnaeus in Lapp
costume
(painting by
Martin Hoffmann,
1737)

ad Italium.

VIRO NOBILISSIMO ET CONSULTISSIMO
D. GEORGIO CLIFFORTIO J. V. D.

Frontispiece of *Flora Lapponica* (Amsterdam, 1737)

Linnaeus as bridegroom (painting by J.H. Scheffel, 1739)

Sara Elisabeth Moraea, Linnaeus's bride

Uppsala, 1770 (engraving by F. Akrel)

CAROLI LINNÆI
Archiat. Reg. & Med. ac Botan Prof. Upsal.
Naturæ Curioforum DIOSCORIDIS secundi,

MATERIA MEDICA,

LIBER I. DE PLANTIS.

Secundum

Genera,	Differentias,	Synonyma,
Loca,	Durationes,	Culturas,
Nomina,	Simplicia,	Præparata,
Qualitates,	Modos,	Potentias,
Vires,	Usus,	Composita.

Digestus.

Cum Privilegio S. R. M.tis Suec. & S. R. M.tis Polon. ac Elector. Saxon.

HOLMIÆ,
Typis ac sumptibus LAURENTII SALVII,
Anno 1749.

Linnaeus's coat of arms, showing his favorite plant *Linnaea borealis*

(Top left) Frontispiece and title page of *Materia medica*
(Stockholm, 1749)
(Bottom left) Linnaeus's estate at Hammarby (engraving from
Egenhändiga anteckningar af Carl Linnaeus,
edited by Adam Afzelius, Stockholm, 1823)

85

Linnaeus in 1775 (engraving after the portrait by Alexander Roslin)

Part Two

CAREER AND INFLUENCE

8

"God's Registrar"

Though Linnaeus is best known as a great botanist, what predominates in his scientific life-work is not a subject but a method. He advanced the descriptive-comparative examination of the vegetable and animal kingdoms in a unique fashion and brought the static view of living nature to its highest point. Hence an account of his career logically begins with his accomplishments as a systematizer.

As has been said, Linnaeus believed that in making an inventory and an orderly arrangement of all the realms of nature he was executing a divine commission. He has been described very aptly as "God's Registrar,"[1] a term which was intended to indicate not only his consciousness of a mission but his preëminent ability in the working techniques of listing and classification. Linnaeus was fitted for this task by a keen eye for the processes and forms of nature, a knack for quickly and accurately recognizing similarities and connections, and a genuine love of collecting. He became aware of this while still young, and throughout his working life he always knew where his greatest strength lay. "He always proved himself a born methodicus," he wrote of himself: "he was one of the keenest observers we have had; therefore he was an author, not a compiler."[2]

Knowledge of a large number of animals or plants must in itself lead, if only for practical reasons, to an arrangement of them according to some sort of system, whether by their striking or important characteristics or by the sort of usefulness they have for man. The earliest scientific classification of objects in nature was made by Aristotle in the fourth century B.C., and the principles he established retained their authority well into the sixteenth century and even into the seventeenth. They proved adequate enough, since the number of known animals and plants did not increase substantially over the intervening period. Interest in nature received new impetus during the Renaissance through the rediscovery of the intellectual world of ancient Greece, but it was the discovery of new continents and regions, with many hitherto unknown animals and plants, that showed the necessity for a comprehensive arrangement and classification. Until then, plants had been considered mainly for their usefulness as food, and especially as medicine, but other points of view now developed. The great herbals that had been compiled, principally in the sixteenth century, by the "fathers of botany" (Otto Brunfels, 1530–36; Hieronymous Bock, 1539; Leonhard Fuchs, 1542) contain almost nothing but descriptions of plants, often accompanied by illustrations, sometimes in alphabetical order (Fuchs) but mostly put down helterskelter.

The French physician and botanist Charles de L'Escluse (Carolus Clusius, 1526–1609) was the first to extend the study of plants beyond their properties as food and medicine and to group them according to the characteristics of their place of origin, as for instance the alpine flora. In the great botanical work *De plantis* [Concerning Plants] (1583) by Andrea Cesalpino (1519–1603), the papal physician who gained fame through his anatomical-physiological studies of the circulation of the blood, 1500 species are described, almost 1000 more than had been known by Aristotle's pupil Theophrastus (370–285 B.C.). Cesalpino divided plants into trees, bushes, and herbs, as had been customary since Aristotle, but he added a classification based on the appearance of flowers and fruit. Thus he took the first step toward building a system which, in the light of further developments, must be described as artificial, a distinction destined to play a considerable role in botany in contrast to zoology.* However, in view of his very strong bent toward anatomical and physiological studies of plants, Cesalpino was probably aiming for a "natural" arrangement.[3] Independently of him, the Swiss botanist Caspar Bauhin (1560–1624) undertook a critical review of all the plant names known up to his time and arranged plants according to far-reaching similarities of their outer forms. Bauhin can therefore be regarded as the founder of natural plant taxonomy. Bauhin gave the first descriptions of numerous plants and was acquainted with about 6000 species in all. In his work, too, there is an intimation of binary nomenclature—the designation of a plant by its generic name and its specific name.

Zoology was also inherited from Aristotle, who founded the scientific study of animals. He had divided the animal kingdom into animals with circulatory systems, corresponding to vertebrates, and bloodless animals, which in a general way correspond to invertebrates.[4] Conrad Gesner (1516–1565), the Swiss scholar who also made great contributions to botany, published a large number of his own observations in his *Historia animalium* [An Account of Animals] (1550), a work that marks the beginning of modern zoology.

From these beginnings systematic biology developed. Simultaneously new knowledge in anatomy and physiology, in zoology and in botany, constantly revealed more and more of the inner structure and function of living organisms. In this way the recognition and separation of new species were continously advanced. Aiding in the work were the botanical gardens laid out here and there as early as the sixteenth century, first in Italy and then in Germany and Holland.

* As defined in *Taxonomy of Vascular Plants* by G.H.M. Lawrence (New York: Macmillan, 1951): "An artificial system classifies organisms for convenience, primarily as an aid to identification and usually by means of one or a few characters. A natural system reflects the situation as it is believed to exist in nature and utilizes all information available at the time."—Ed.

Most important of all, the seventeenth century brought a large number of new morphological observations, thanks principally to the use of the microscope. By comparison, advances in taxonomy were meager. Mention should be made, however, of the trail-blazing works of Joachim Jung (Jungius, 1587–1657), a secondary-school principal in Hamburg, whose works were published by his pupils after his death. In his *Isagoge phytoscopia* [Introduction to the Observation of Plants] he laid down very precise rules for the description of plants and made tables for the purpose of conciseness. The German botanist August Quirinus Rivinus (1652–1723), like Jungius before him, discarded the old division into trees, bushes, and herbs; he also made contributions as a taxonomist. His artificial system was based on the construction of the corolla, and he proposed the use of binomials, though he did not consistently employ them himself.

The British pastor and naturalist John Ray (1627–1705), with his wealthy friend Francis Willughby (1635–1672), who was an enthusiastic amateur botanist, undertook research journeys through England and the continent to gather material for a great joint work about all living things. After Willughby's untimely death, the compilation and publication of the findings were carried on by Ray alone. In botany he built a system based on the structure and appearance of fruits, flowers, leaves, and other organs, thus taking into account the greatest possible number of similarities and therefore forming a natural system. Ray distinguished plants without flowers from those that had them, and among the latter those with one and two seed leaves—monocotyledons and dicotyledons. He was also at pains to find the most exact possible definition of the concept of species, and he regarded as the safest criterion of species (which he considered unalterable) similarity of offspring. Probably the most striking thing about Ray's zoological writings is the absence of the fabulous animals, which were still to be found in the works of Conrad Gesner and his followers. It is justifiable to call Ray the founder of taxonomy as an independent branch of biology.

In contrast to this system with its cryptogams, monocotyle-

dons, and dicotyledons, the system of Joseph Pitton de Tournefort is an unmistakable departure from the principle of
natural organization. Based on the structure of the corolla
alone, it was characterized by its simplicity and ease in use,
it spread quickly and enjoyed remarkable popularity. In this
case an artificial system was able to gain recognition, even
though the tendency seemed to be toward a more natural
arrangement. However, Tournefort by his definition of the
concept of genus had rendered an important and lasting
contribution to taxonomy. He was the immediate predecessor of Linnaeus, who, as mentioned earlier, had learned of
Tournefort's work from Rothman and described it in his
Classes plantarum:

> He was the first to create a sound method of division into
> classes, orders, genera, and species; and he introduced
> every genus under one and the same name, something
> Raius [Ray] did not concern himself with. Tournefort col-
> lected 11,200 species, though the number shrank to about
> half that, to be sure, with varieties subtracted. But he
> lacked a sure distinction of species; also he was wrong in
> separating trees and bushes. His method is above all very
> carefully worked out with good characterizations and
> well-distinguished genera, but it contributed more in set-
> tling the design of flowers of each genus than in descrip-
> tion.[5]

The zoological system of the German naturalist Jacob
Theodor Klein (1685–1759) was also artificial. The author, a
city magistrate in Danzig, was passionately devoted to natural science. His system was based on the form, number, and
position of the limbs and neglected the marks of natural
relationships among animals so grossly that its rejection was
inevitable. It can be regarded as the work of an amateur
who persisted in dwelling on externals, and his attacks on
Linnaeus's *Systema naturae* as those of a zealot. Nevertheless, the eccentricity of Klein's system, contrary to his intention, contributed substantially to the advancement of
Linnaeus's work.

This brief survey of the development of taxonomy before
Linnaeus, and of his more famous predecessors, provides a
yardstick for evaluating what was accomplished under his
influence. However, before discussing Linnaeus as taxonomist and creator of the sexual system of classification, the
discovery of sexuality in plants must be described. In the
sixteenth and seventeenth centuries it was merely to express
with especial vividness the difference in appearance of plants
that individual botanists talked about male and female
plants. In 1682, the London doctor Nehemiah Grew, on
purely theoretical grounds, assumed sexual reproduction in
plants; for the experimental proof, credit is due to
Camerarius. He used the herb mercury *(Mercuralis annua),*
a member of the Euphorbiaceae [spurge family], separating
the plants with only male flowers from those with only
female flowers—that is, those with only stamens from others
with only pistils. Later he carried on experiments with other
plants, and in his work *De sexu plantarum epistola* [Letter
concerning the Sex of Plants] (1694) he founded the teaching
of the sexuality of plants. Through the French botanist Sebastian Vaillant, Linnaeus became acquainted with and supported Camerarius's theory. In 1702 the German doctor Johann Heinrich Burkhard at Wolfenbüttel proposed that the
number and arrangement of the stamens and the pistils be
used as the basis of an artificial system of plants.

Compared with what his predecessors accomplished, Linnaeus's work as a taxonomist is most impressive. It had great
consistency of structure; it produced an overwhelming en-
richment of nomenclature; it was successful and well liked as
a simple and practical method for naming plants, which because of this system, became the chief occupation of botanists. For a proper appreciation of Linnaeus's achievements,
one must remember that he was almost entirely self-taught.
The instruction from his father, in school, and at the universities of Lund and Uppsala showed him the way to literary
sources, which were made directly accessible to him through
his teachers Rothman, Stobaeus, and Olof Celsius. Linnaeus
studied Tournefort's system and based his early work on the
sexuality of plants (1730) on the experimental results of

Camerarius, without adding any further experiments. At this time he was already beginning, as he himself writes, "to doubt that the Tournefort system was adequate, and so decided to describe all flowers, put them in new classes, reform the names and families in an entirely novel fashion, something that demanded time and almost did away with sleep."[6]

The idea of constructing a system based on the sex organs of plants certainly occurred to Linnaeus without knowledge of the ideas expressed by Burkhard. Very early Linnaeus had recognized the meaning of stamens and pistils as regular, constituent parts of every flower, and he could not imagine that any change could take place in these most important plant organs. This was the chief reason for his making the sexual organs of plants the foundation of his system, even when their minuteness sometimes made it impossible to distinguish them with the naked eye. The system was expressly described by him as a sexual system; he regarded it as artificial although individual classes and orders met the requirements of a natural classification. They are *natural* in the sense defined by him.[7] This holds good for the Rosaceae, the Papilionatae, the Orchidaceae, and the Coniferae. Indeed, Linnaeus himself pointed out in *Genera plantarum* the identity of his classes 14 through 20 with the natural classes of earlier botanists.[8] In the beginning he was convinced of the unalterability of species, but later he developed doubts about the universal application of this concept. In his writings about the appearance of hybrids he recognizes the emergence of new forms through cross-breeding as continuing creation in accordance with divine laws.

The first signs of the preliminary work for his own system are recognizable in the various versions of *Hortus Uplandicus* written around 1730.* These show a gradual departure from Tournefort's system and the development of Linnaeus's own principles of organization. At first the work looked exactly like a catalogue, but in the later manuscripts the con-

---

* Three manuscripts with the title *Hortus Uplandicus* and one entitled *Adonis Uplandicus sive Hortus Uplandicus* have been preserved; these were first published in 1888 in a single volume.—Ed.

cept of species is more clearly defined in that varieties (in color) no longer stand as separate species. Also new names appear, such as the genus *Helianthus,* which earlier botanists had designated as *Helenium, Helianthemum,* and *Heliotropicum,* and the name *Rudbeckia* which Linnaeus coined and which marks the beginning of the custom, which later became habitual with him, of using the names of famous botanists, sometimes contemporaries, in his system. Linnaeus was bestowing an honor when he utilized the family names of his colleagues, and he knew how to make adroit use of the vanity of friends and enemies. Frequently he had the pleasure of receiving formal requests for the use of a proper name in his system. For instance, his pupil Johann Andreas Murray, then professor of medicine and botany in Göttingen, asked for this honor, and Linnaeus replied by letter with the comforting assurance that he would "certainly find a plant for him."[9] The most important development, however, appears for the first time in the third version of *Hortus Uplandicus* (1731) under the heading *Classium distributio* [Distribution of Classes]: the sexual system with twenty-one classes; in the version entitled *Adonis Uplandicus sive Hortus Uplandicus* he extends his arrangement to twenty-four classes. In so doing, Linnaeus, at the age of twenty-three had laid the foundation for the building of his system.

His fundamental work *Systema naturae* divides nature, following Aristotelian practice, into three kingdoms. The division into mineral, plant, and animal kingdoms is made according to these determining characteristics: "Stones grow; plants grow and live; animals grow, live, and feel."[10] This work, which can fairly be described as the laws of natural scientific taxonomy, came from the press in a fairly large edition at two and a half florins, and it remains today one of the great bibliophilic treasures. Its publication was first mentioned December 9, 1735, in the *Hamburgische Berichte.* The authorship of the review was not established until 1919.[11] Linnaeus himself, in a letter of August 1 from Harderwijk, had drawn attention to his own work: "This famous medicus, a born researcher of natural things, has given to the printer his *Systema naturae* which presents the three kingdoms of

nature. . . . The author has included uncommonly many observations in so few pages."

Whereas the first edition was printed in large folio format,
the later ones were brought out in the more convenient
octavo size. The second edition, 1740, was published by G.
Kiesewetter, Stockholm, and ran to 80 pages. Altogether
thirteen editions appeared, twelve of them during Linnaeus's lifetime.[12]

There is no doubt that Linnaeus had a great preference for
his classification of the plant kingdom, and his reputation as
a taxonomist in this field is so great that one is justified in
departing from Linnaeus's own sequence and beginning
with a discussion of the *Regnum vegetabile.*

In accordance with the key supplied by Linnaeus his system is arranged as follows:[13]

I. *Flowering Plants*

A. Flowers hermaphrodites with stamens and pistils

  a. With free stamens

    aa. With stamens of irregular length

Class 1	(1 stamen)	MONANDRIA
Class 2	(2 stamens)	DIANDRIA
Class 3	(3 stamens)	TRIANDRIA
Class 4	(4 stamens)	TETRANDIA
Class 5	(5 stamens)	PENTANDRIA
Class 6	(6 stamens)	HEXANDRIA
Class 7	(7 stamens)	HEPTANDRIA
Class 8	(8 stamens)	OCTANDRIA
Class 9	(9 stamens)	ENNEANDRIA
Class 10	(10 stamens)	DECANDRIA
Class 11	(12–19 stamens)	DODECANDRIA
Class 12	(20 or more stamens attached to the inner side of the calyx)	ICOSANDRIA
Class 13	(20 to 1000 stamens)	POLYANDRIA

Class 14	(4 stamens, of which 2 adjacent ones exceed the other 2 in size)	DIDYNAMIA
Class 15	(6 stamens, 4 exceeding the other, 2 in length, the 2 shorter ones positioned opposite each other)	TETRADYNAMIA

b. Stamens united to each other or to the pistil

Class 16	(stamens united by their filaments)	MONADELPHIA
Class 17	(stamens united by their filaments into 2 groups)	DIADELPHIA
Class 18	(stamens united by their filaments into 3 or more groups)	POLYDELPHIA
Class 19	(stamens united by their anthers which form a cylinder)	SYNGENESIA
Class 20	(stamens attached to the pistil)	GYNANDRIA

B. Flowers unisexual, or if hermaphroditic, present with unisexual flowers on the same plant

Class 21	(male and female flowers on a single plant)	MONOECIA
Class 22	(male and female flowers on different plants)	DIOECIA
Class 23	(bisexual flowers as well as male and/or female flowers on a single plant)	POLYGAMIA

II. *Plants Lacking Flowers*

Class 24	(flowers concealed in the fruit, or hidden from our eyes by their minuteness)	CRYPTOGAMIA

With this system Linnaeus handed the botanist "the Ariadne thread" by which he could find his way through the bewildering labyrinth of the plant world.

"The Ariadne thread in botany is classification, without which there is chaos." This sentence from *Fundamenta botanica*[14] also demonstrates Linnaeus's belief that the systematic arrangement of the plant world was a necessary prerequisite to further discoveries. This point of view, which may rightly be called symptomatic of the times, showed him the direction for his scientific work. How closely he stuck to this path is proved by a glance at his other botanical writings. In the same year as *Fundamenta botanica*, there also appeared *Bibliotheca botanica,* a list of the most important titles in botanical literature. As in the *Fundamenta,* Linnaeus was at work on a theory of plant taxonomy in the *Critica botanica,* dedicated to Dillenius, in *Genera plantarum,* and in *Classes plantarum.* All three works appeared in Holland, the first two in 1737, *Classes plantarum* a year later. This last book, which he dedicated to the governors of the provinces of Dalecarlia and Västerbotten, offers a comparison of the plant systems in use up to then, and with its synoptical arrangement affords in a compass of 657 pages convincing proof that Linnaeus's great gift for systematic classification extended to scientific literature as well.

The further elaboration of his plant system is recorded in the later editions of *Systema naturae* and in *Species plantarum,* published in 1753 in two volumes with a total of 1200 pages and a detailed index. Linnaeus considered the latter his most significant work, and with reason, for it demonstrates the unique richness of his observations. These were based on living plants at the Botanical Garden in Uppsala, those that he had seen on his journeys, the ones he had raised from seed sent to him by botanists outside Sweden; as well as on the dried and pressed plants which he received in trade or as gifts from many parts of the world, many from his own pupils. His herbarium finally attained an abundance that was hardly equaled in his time. But another special kind of importance attaches to *Species plantarum:* in it for the first time a consistent nomenclature with binomials was used.

For an example of the desirability of shortening plant designations, take the name of the European red currant, which Bauhin called *Grossularia, multiplici acino: seu non spinosa hortensis rubra, seu Ribes officinarium.* This was a description for purposes of identifying the species rather than a scientific name. The pressing need for shortening names of plants had been recognized by botanists before Linnaeus, and a certain number of changes in this direction had been made. However, Linnaeus's consistent use of dou-

ble names—binomial nomenclature—went appreciably further. Each species that became known to him was given this
sort of double name, of which the first (generic) part specified
the genus, and the second (specific) part was derived from
the principal point of difference (*differentia*) from other
plants of the same genus. These second names, specific epi-
thets, usually adjectival, Linnaeus also called *nomina trivialia* ["convenient names"]. This kind of nomenclature,
which corresponds essentially to the way people are com-
monly identified by given names and family names, obviously affords the botanist great advantages. The red currant
was now called simply *Ribes rubrum*, the improvement on
the old name being so obvious and so self-explanatory that
the general application of the principle has earned the distinction of making the plant kingdom orderly and comprehensible.

"He was the first to define the species of plants by reliable
differentiae," and "He was the first to introduce *nomina
trivialia* in the whole of natural history": these are autobiographical notes[15] commenting on what he believed to be a
genuine advance and, as he repeatedly observed, he was
convinced of the lasting nature of his contribution. Recognition of his method in Sweden and abroad was not slow in
coming, and the multiplicity of botanical works written according to his principles was proof that he had followed the
right road.

In a letter to Bäck in 1762, he said: "Now the whole world
is obsessed with writing in the field of botany, now they can
get ahead without difficulty, thanks to my method; I cannot
manage to read as fast as they publish; then I have to fit all
this into my system."[16]

In his zoological system Linnaeus paid far more attention
to natural relationships than in his arrangement of the plant
kingdom. He divided the animal kingdom into six classes,
which even in the first edition of *Systema naturae* were

sometimes distinguished from one another through important criteria:

I. *Quadrupeds*
   Hairy body. Four feet. Females viviparous, milk-producing.

II. *Birds*
   Feathered body. Two wings. Two feet. Bony beak. Females oviparous.

III. *Amphibia*
   Body naked or scaly. No molar teeth; others always present. No feathers.

IV. *Fishes*
   Body footless, possessing real fins, naked or scaly.

V. *Insects*
   Body covered with bony shell instead of skin. Head equipped with antennae.

VI. *Worms*
   Body muscles attached at a single point to a quasi-solid base.

The classes of the quadrupeds and the birds correspond to the divisions still used today. The amphibian class included reptiles. In the class of worms, however, Linnaeus included all the animals that could not be fitted into the other classes. Thus to Class VI belong, together with conchs and shellfish, the cuttlefish *(Sepia)*, the medusas *(Medusa)*, the sea urchins *(Echinus)*, and finally microorganisms with the description: "Body covering various and heterogeneous."

The inclusion of man in the animal kingdom in the first edition of *Systema naturae* called forth loud protest from many contemporaries. Linnaeus had placed him in the highest position. In Class I, Quadrupeds, under the order of Anthropomorpha, the first genus mentioned is *Homo;* and Linnaeus, in place of a specific designation, simply put the exhortation: *Nosce te ipsum* [Know thyself]. The sloth is also placed among the Anthropomorpha, no doubt on account of its apelike appearance, climbing ability, and, importantly, the presence of mammary glands. But this error does not detract from the importance of the first lines of *Regnum animale* [Animal Kingdom], which show Linnaeus's recognition of the relationship between men and apes. Later[17] he described the first order of mammals as primates and provided a striking description of the species *Homo sapiens.* In this he was so far ahead of his contemporaries that his point of view did not find general acceptance until more than a century later, in connection with the theory of evolution.

In the further elaboration of his system of nature, Linnaeus made more fundamental changes in the arrangement of the animal kingdom than in the *Regnum vegetabile;* later editions of the latter were steadily enlarged to include and classify newly discovered plants, but the system of the animal kingdom was repeatedly improved.

Subsequent editions of *Systema naturae* show no particular advances over the first until the tenth edition (1758), which is impressive not only for its substantially broader presentation and the introduction of binomial nomenclature but for the appraisal of much new material. The degree to which Linnaeus's work had given impetus to the cataloguing of the animal kingdom, and the discovery of new species in Sweden as well as abroad, are shown by the increase in the number of animal forms in the successive editions of *Systema naturae.* Thus in 1735 only 549 species are mentioned; in the seventh edition the number had risen to 1174; in the tenth to 4387, and in the following edition, the zoological part of which appeared in 1766, there were 5897. Many new species were described by Linnaeus himself, as is shown in the text of *Fauna suecia* [Swedish Animals] (1746). Even more species, however, were added through the descriptions by other authors throughout the world. The abundance of material supplied him enabled Linnaeus to rework his animal system, although inevitably here and there a new species was wrongly classified because the description was imprecise or inadequate. The tenth edition is properly accounted the most important for the development of animal taxonomy. Here the class of mammals is for the first time designated as *Mammalia;* since Linnaeus now counted whales among the mammals, he had to give up the designation *Quadrupedia.* Though the mammalian characteristics of whales had been known to naturalists earlier, Linnaeus was the first to recognize their relationship openly. This edition is still regarded as the foundation of zoological nomenclature, just as *Species plantarum* (1753) is considered the starting point for botanical nomenclature.

If one compares Linnaeus's animal and plant systems, a fundamental difference is immediately apparent, which also explains the more natural character of the animal system. For botany, the sexual system afforded a practical key, simple to use and valid in itself. In *Regnum animalium,* on the other hand, there was need for different principles of arrangement in the various groups, sometimes based on a single organ, sometimes on several. Thus Linnaeus came closer to the actual relationships and the various species of animals, even though he did seem to rely more than need be upon individual organs and specific characteristics. However, in classifying the animal kingdom, Linnaeus was principally interested in practical applicability, in the process of cataloguing as such, to which he attributed great significance for the understanding of all phenomena of the animal and plant kingdoms.

Linnaeus's efforts to bring the mineral kingdom into one system as well had the least permanent effect, even though he also achieved certain accomplishments in this field. His *Regnum lapideum* [Mineral Kingdom], translated from the first edition of *Systema naturae,* was as follows:

A. Rocks, or simple stones
    Order 1. Glassy
              Genera: flint, quartz, silica
    Order 2. Calcareous
              Genera: marble, spar, schist

Order 3.   Incombustible
Genera: mica, talcum, ollaris, aminanthus,
asbestos

B.   Minerals, or composite rocks
Order 1.   Salts
Genera: natron, niter, muria, alum,
vitriol
Order 2.   Sulphurs
Genera: amber, bitumen, pyrites,
arsenic
Order 3.   Mercuries
Genera: hydragyrum, antinomy, bismuth,
zinc, iron, tin, copper, silver, gold

C.   Fossils, or aggregated rocks
Order 1.   Earths
Genera: gravels, clays, humus, ocher,
margarite.
Order 2.   Compounded
Order 3.   Petrified

The division of inorganic nature into stones, metals, sulfurs, and salts, which can be traced as far back as the Arab physician and naturalist Avicenna (980–1037) is to be found in Linnaeus's arrangement of the mineral kingdom in the first and second classes of his system. For his principle of classification in class A, dealing with rocks, Linnaeus chose their behavior in fire, thereby following the proposals of earlier naturalists.[18] In the classification glassy he put the rocks that melt into glass, in calcareous those that fall into powder, and in incombustible, those that are not affected by fire. It is completely in accord with the knowledge of the times that minerals are classified together with rocks. Moreover, Linnaeus's mineral system has as its basis of classification the practical use of objects from the inorganic world. That this view was shared by Linnaeus's contemporaries is proved by the work of Johann Gottschalk Wallerius which appeared in 1768. In it, the external features, including place of origin and usefulness, are given great importance, while behavior in fire and in the presence of chemical reagents are relegated to a secondary position. A critical appraisal of Linnaeus's significance for mineralogy shows that in this field he belongs to the older school, which even in his lifetime was being abandoned, especially through the influence of Swedish naturalists, notably Axel Frederic Cronstedt (1722–1765). Because crystallography was then developing along geometrical lines and the growth of chemistry was bringing new knowledge, the systematic view of the mineral kingdom gained new principles of organization.

Nothing is more natural than that Linnaeus should have interested himself in classifying illnesses too. As early as his student years he encountered nosological systems, which had been of increasing interest among doctors since the seventeenth century. The beginnings of such systems go back to the Athenian physician Mnesitheos in the third century B.C. From him comes the classification of sicknesses according to their nature and their characteristic development.[19] Modern nosology begins with the Swiss physician Felix Platter (1536–1614). The great British doctor Thomas Sydenham (1626–1689) pointed to the example of the botanists, though he worked out no system of his own. He expected that the systematizing of illnesses would result in increased interest in observing the patient and thereby determining the way the disease habitually developed, and from this a formulation of specific therapeutic methods. Sydenham's ideas were seized upon by a professor of medicine in Montpellier, François Boissier Sauvages de Lacroix, who has been mentioned as one of Linnaeus's correspondents. In 1731 Sauvages published the foundations of his nosology, which followed exactly the example of the botanists.

Linnaeus early became interested in the writings of Sauvages, in whom he immediately recognized an accomplished taxonomist. They began to correspond, and in Linnaeus's letters and through his own work in natural-science taxonomy he again and again gave encouragement to Sauvages.

The relationship between the two like-minded scholars developed into a true friendship, and presumably it was due to the influence of Sauvages that Linnaeus's interest in medicine never abated. Without question Linnaeus got from Sauvages the first urge toward involvement in nosology. In the beginning he followed Sauvages's classification, but gradually, with his own broadening experience in medicine and his deepening interest in the task, his own system emerged. This was published in 1759 as a doctoral dissertation and four years later brought out under his own name with the title *Genera morborum.* In the foreword he declares that there had been no proper classification of diseases

> until the famous Professor Sauvages of Montpellier, an ornament to France and to the entire world, published a complete *systema morborum* which, according to my view, through its natural classification, description of symptoms, and completeness, so far excels all other systems that none can be compared with it. For more than twenty years I have used it in teaching at the University of Uppsala, and year after year through new observations have improved it until it now has assumed the form that I am presenting in this book.

The didactic importance of nosology should not be underestimated, or the impetus it gave, in Sydenham's sense, to a more careful observation of symptoms. In the following decades still further classifications of this sort emerged (by R. A. Vogel, W. Cullen, D. Macbridge, C. G. Seller, F. L. Banz, among others), in which the influence of Linnaeus's principles of taxonomy is unmistakable. But, just as the importance of systems in botany and zoology declined in the nineteenth century, so did that of nosology, as more and more was found out about the inner processes of illness. Symptoms became less significant, a development that corresponded to the abandonment of classification by single characteristics in the other natural sciences and a transition to so-called natural principles.

The great creator of systems, Linnaeus, had strong influence in other fields too, as for instance the *Linnaeismus graphicus* (The Application of Natural-History Classifications to the Classification of Documents). This paleographic system was devised by the Göttingen historian Johann Christoph Gatterer, who published it in 1765. However, it quickly proved unsuited to diplomacy and was replaced by other principles of classification. A system of geography by the same author fared no better.

The construction of scientific systems could also become a passion or an amusement. Linnaeus himself proved this by devising a list of "Officers of Flora's Army," in which he assigned military ranks to some of his colleagues, thus revealing his view of their merits as botanists. This list, which he made up in about 1752, is headed by "General Linnaeus," with the names of his strongest supporters following as chief officers. The lowest rank was assigned to Johann G. Siegesbeck, who, in 1737, had been particularly severe in his criticism of Linnaeus's sexual system, declaring that " 'such loathsome harlotry' as several males to one female would never have been permitted in the vegetable kingdom by the Creator" and asking "how anyone could teach without offence 'so licentious a method' to studious youth."[20]

Anyone who knows anything about taxonomy before Linnaeus will acknowledge without hesitation the great importance of his systematic writings for the development of the natural sciences in the eighteenth century. Neither the outgrowths and exaggerations that his followers and his opponents added to his system nor the elevation of his views to dogmas by some contemporaries and later scholars—which always has a crippling effect on the development of the natural sciences—could alter the slightest the fact that his work as a taxonomist marks an epoch in the history of science. As for his influence in later periods, one must remember that his own conversion to natural systems pointed the way which in his time was supported more by experience and simple observation than by real knowledge. But if one thinks, too, about the vast number of animal and plant names he devised and the number of them still in use today, his enduring influence becomes veritable fact. It is recognized throughout the world that an "L" attached to the name of a plant establishes his authorship. A visitor to any botanical garden can verify this, and it is no wonder that even today Linnaeus still enjoys popularity as a naturalist. It was as a taxonomist that he became famous and will remain so, but he made contributions as a naturalist as well, and these have generally received less recognition.

9

Investigator of Nature

That Linnaeus was a naturalist
in "the modern sense" was seriously questioned by Julius von
Sachs in his famous *History of Botany* (1875). But T. M. Fries,
in his biography of Linnaeus (1903), pointed out that it would
be hard to name another botanist who carried on such varied
studies of the plant world.[1] In recent decades more attention
has been paid than was earlier the case to Linnaeus's work
on the anatomical, physiological, and geographical problems
connected with plants. His investigation of the sexuality of
plants and his descriptive contributions led him very early to
anatomical studies, and he made a number of individual observations.[2] His most important contributions to plant physiology, including experimental work, have to do, naturally
enough, with processes of fertilization. But his lectures on
botany, which have been preserved in auditors' transcripts
and dissertations, and his observations in travel journals and
letters show how great was his interest in botany in general,
not simply in taxonomy. The importance of his work is probably easier to judge today than it was for his contemporaries,
and perhaps even for the nineteenth century. Two examples
of this are his researches into the appearance of mutations,
and into the formation of the rings in trees and their depen-

dence upon climate. He deserves credit, too, as the first to examine high-mountain flora with respect to ecology, boundaries, and plant associations, and no less for his studies on the periodic life phases of plants and their movements.[3]

His works on the characteristics and cultivation of economically important plants substantially increased the public interest in botany and in natural science in general. It was, in fact, at the instigation of the Hats party that the government and the Diet were particularly receptive to practical measures to advance the native economy and were also eager to fashion an independent foreign commercial policy. In this connection Linnaeus's economic work had great practical significance for the public weal and it deserved support, as he emphasized again and again with adroitness and vigor. If one considers how much people in the eighteenth century, in Sweden and in other European countries, interested themselves in the cultivation of tobacco, silkworms, olive trees, mulberry bushes, and plants for dyes, then Linnaeus's utilitarian natural history accords wholly with the spirit of the times.

As early as 1740 his paper about the value of natural science for the national economy appeared in the transactions of the Academy of Sciences, and eight years later he published a dissertation entitled *Flora oeconomica*. The latter was written in Swedish, which was appropriate to its practical purpose: that of recognizing and exploiting the importance of Sweden's wild plants for her native economy. In 1752 Linnaeus had a dissertation about domestic plants published, and he himself published in 1757 a work about the possibility of making bread from native plants when there was a shortage of grain.

At the time of his visit to Holland, he had recognized that the cultivation of tea would have great economic importance. But his efforts to acclimatize in Sweden tea bushes from east Asia were not crowned with success. The importation of tea into Europe was increasing by leaps and bounds, and although Linnaeus himself was no great friend of tea drinking, he was nevertheless at pains on his return to Sweden to acquire seeds or young seedlings of tea plants. Although he had reported in *Hortus Cliffortianus* the failure of attempts to cultivate tea in the botanical garden at Hartekamp, he considered further attempts as hopeful. After a number of failures, Captain Carl Gustaf Ekeberg of the Swedish East India Company succeeded in 1763 in bringing a large number of tea plants to Göteborg.[4] The first shipment of these plants withered on the way to Uppsala, and the remainder were brought by the captain's wife in a coach. She is said to have held the heavy chest on her knees during the whole trip to avoid damage to the plants. Linnaeus was overjoyed. When he had first heard of the arrival of the living plants in Göteborg he had written to Captain Ekeberg in the greatest excitement: "Truly, if this is tea, I will see to it that your name has greater fame than that of Alexander the Great."[5] In his autobiographical reminiscences he celebrates the occasion with this statement:

> Finally Linnaeus received tea, alive, from China, something he had wanted for years, something no one before him had succeeded in accomplishing, for neither seeds nor roots tolerate transportation. Linnaeus had given directions that immediately on departure from China the seeds should be placed in earth and then watered as if in a hotbed. This was done, and God so blessed him in this undertaking that he was the first to have the honor to see tea brought alive by Ekeberg to Europe. He considered nothing more important than to shut the doors through which all the silver from Europe flows away.[6]

Linnaeus used Captain Ekeberg's name for the plant *Ekebergia* and thus rewarded him after his own fashion. In 1765 two of the successfully imported tea plants were still alive, and Linnaeus had great hopes of continuing to keep them so. In the same year he had a dissertation about tea, *Potus theae*, published, in which he described his efforts. When finally only a single plant was left, Linnaeus gave up hope of being able to acclimatize tea plants in Sweden.

He took an active part in a search for native plants that would serve as tea substitutes, working on the hypothesis that drinks similar in taste and appearance could be achieved. On the other hand, he did not expect from any native plant the enlivening and stimulating effect of tea. He also made suggestions for the cultivation of plants that might produce oil and dyes. At his instigation the common couch grass was taken into consideration as food for pigs and even, in time of need, as human nourishment.[7]

His work in the animal section of his system also led to anatomical and physiological studies. Pointing in his autobiographical notes to the way in which he had revealed the multiplicity of forms in the animal world, he added:

> By himself he discovered more than all who had lived before him; he was the first to give generic and specific descriptions of them by the most natural methods. Knowledge of insects and their characterisitics must be credited to him; not to mention the convenient method he invented of recognizing fish by their scales, shellfish by the pattern of their shells, and reptiles by their coverings. He placed whales among the mammals, swimming animals among the amphibians, and removed worms from among the insects.[8]

His contributions to general zoology are almost more completely hidden in his systematic works than are those to botany. But his descriptions of species are frequently so short that the anatomical or physiological basis for the classification of the genus is sometimes not clear. Meaningful and realistic, however, are the accounts of forms newly described by him or published in monographs issued as dissertations, as for example the house dog *Canis familiaris* (1735) and the sheep *Ovis* (1754). He even instituted behavioral studies of household animals and wild birds and described them vividly.[9] His observations of migratory birds and his views about the cause of the migration of birds and his views about the cause of the migration of birds are as worthy of attention as his attempts to cultivate pearls in the river mussels in the Fyrisån, the stream that flows through Uppsala.[10]

It is true that much of what Linnaeus accomplished in the

realm of general biology was dictated by concern for taxonomy, and the principle of usefulness he so often stressed was from the start a strong incentive to explore the creations and phenomena of nature. The manysidedness of his work indicates that he was a universal naturalist, an impression still further strengthened by consideration of his medical activities and careful study of his travel reports.

10

Physician and Teacher of Medicine

Some attention has already been given to Linnaeus's activities as physician and a professor of medicine and, among his achievements as a taxonomist, to his attempts at a classification of diseases. A glance at the results of recent Linnaean research shows that since the fundamental works of Otto E. A. Hjelt many important findings about this aspect of his work have been published, though until now they have not been sufficiently taken into account by his biographers. Publicly, in his own time, in contrast to his departmental colleague, the admirably knowledgeable and greatly gifted clinician Nils Rosén, Linnaeus was less conspicuous for medical achievements. And yet, especially on questions of drugs and nutrition, he was recognized as an expert, made many important contributions in lectures and writings, and above all kept track of foreign publications, appraising them with reference to the state of knowledge in Sweden. He himself, as is evident from his autobiographical notes, considered his medical activities and his abilities as a doctor no less important than the rest of his scientific work. His autobiographical writings include a statement in tabular form of his accomplishments in the field of medicine,[1] which gives a very good survey, though it again proves that a conclusion based on contemporary knowledge may easily differ from later critical judgments, especially if it has to do with one's own work.

In addition to his own writings on medical themes, including manuscripts only published after his death, the dissertations of his pupils provide a particularly good source of material. Out of 187 such so-called disputations which, according to academic custom, were delivered publicly, 85 deal with medical questions. Their content and wording were actually Linnaeus's, set down by the student. That this was customary is proved by a remark of the Swedish physician Johann Gustaf Acrel in 1796 in a speech about the development of medicine at Uppsala University:

> He [Linnaeus] dictated the dissertations both in Swedish and in Latin, the correction and polishing of the text being left to the candidates; and although he did not concern himself about the Latin, he nevertheless showed his approval when they were well written, and vice versa. To write a disputation, therefore, took barely three hours, for essentially it was simply a lecture on the subject, copied down by the candidate.[2]

Since such disputations discussed new information and experience, often suggested by publications or letters from outside Sweden, more information about Linnaeus's influence as a researcher and teacher of medicine can be derived from them than from his own medical publications.

Linnaeus's first treatment of a medical subject was in the dissertation he submitted in Harderwijk for his M.D. degree. In it, with an adroitness in the handling of the material that reveals the taxonomist, he deals with the symptoms of intermittent fever and explains his new theory about the origin of this disease. His own observations in Sweden, where intermittent fever is frequent in certain regions and in others remarkably rare, had led him to assume that the amount of loam in the soil had a connection with the illness. In his opinion, through drinking water rich in loam, small particles of loam found their way into the blood stream, led to the blockage of small blood vessels, and prevented the elimination of waste matter through the skin, thus causing fever in the body. The high incidence of the disease in Sweden, and especially in Uppsala, is attested to by frequent mention of it in Linnaeus's later writings and letters. Very likely in the majority of cases this was a tertian malaria, which in the eighteenth century was endemic in the whole Baltic region. In a letter to Sauvages,[3] Linnaeus reports a flare-up of the disease in Uppsala, where, in the last three months of 1754, 300 persons fell ill, among them his own wife. Her symptoms are so clearly described that the disease can be diagnosed today as a malarial infection of the tertiary type. As a proven remedy Linnaeus made use of cinchona bark, though he also recommended other measures and medications.

In 1757, in a dissertation entitled *Febris Upsaliensis* [Uppsala Fever] published by the Swedish Linnaean Society in 1959, he described the peculiar circumstances of the appearance of intermittent fever in Uppsala and specifically emphasized the necessity of getting rid of certain pools of dirty, stagnant water within the city limits. This sanitary measure, which he urged upon the police authorities, he regarded as a prerequisite for rooting out the disease. As has been mentioned, he himself came down with intermittent fever in 1764, as did Rosén in 1765. Linnaeus also had an attack in 1767, and according to his reports had had another earlier attack. If one looks critically at the description of the course of these illnesses, the concept of intermittent fever turns out to be a catchall for a number of different contagious illnesses today called respiratory diseases and considered commonplace. In later years Linnaeus moved steadily further away from his loam theory and in a dissertation in 1771 gave a miasmatic explanation of the origin of the disease, attributing it to a change in the outside air, which led to a disturbance of perspiration from the skin.

The ancient Greek physicians, who had a lively interest in the principles of healthy living, created the concept of dietetics, which extended far beyond what is understood by the word today. In the Middle Ages and later too, the rules of dietetics were discussed by doctors and in some cases by

laymen in writings and lectures. These rules were formu-
lated in easily remembered maxims, attributed, probably for
publicity reasons, to the school of Salerno, and reached a
wide audience under the title *Regimen sanitatis Saler-
nitanum* [Salerno Health Régime]. It was through his own
observations in the course of his Lapland journey that Linnaeus became interested in dietetics. He reported: "When I saw
the healthy Lapps I hit upon certain principles through
which men could double the length of their lives, without
sickness and on natural principles."[4]

He then became interested in earlier writings on dietetics
and as material for his lectures, prepared manuscripts which
were later rewritten and enlarged. These manuscripts, and
many lecture notes by his auditors, give a good idea of his
thoughts about the necessity and meaning of a natural way
of life. His manuscript *Lachesis naturalis** and a series of
lecture notes were published in 1907, and a manuscript entitled *Diaeta naturalis* [Natural Diet] was published in 1958.
Both of these are among his literary remains belonging to the
Linnaean Society in London. The first work, dated 1733,
represents the youthful formulation of his dietary views and
is therefore of special interest; above all, it shows that Linnaeus from the beginning considered absolutely necessary a
complete adaptation of man's way of life to the fundamental
laws of nature. Not all of Linnaeus's manuscripts on this
theme are yet in print. Certain sections not included in the
edition of 1907 were found a short time later among the then
unsorted material in the London collection. From these,
which are still unpublished, it is clear that Linnaeus was
constantly making his system more comprehensive; he
added to it the nemesis idea, already mentioned. However,
many of the formulations of his earlier years appear later in
attenuated form. The manuscript of 1733 begins with 136
rules, followed by explanations and examples. Linnaeus re-
lied largely on his own observations, which is one reason that
his lecture course was entitled *Diaeta experimentalis*
[Experimental Diet]. Here is a sampling of his maxims:

* Lachesis in Greek mythology was the one of the three Fates who determined the length of life—Ed.

The newborn should be nourished with mother's milk for
    several years.

Habit is, so to speak, our second nature.

All excess is harmful.

Avoid all evil smells and other impurities in the air.

Perform light physical exercise for as much as one third of
    the day.

Clothes made from the skins of animals are better than
    other kinds.

Man is an animal and should live in accordance with his
    species.

Eat in order to strengthen yourself, not to overburden the
    stomach.

All boiled drinks, including water, are worse than un-
    boiled ones.

Brandy is poison.

Smoking tobacco, snuff, and chewing tobacco are poison.

One must never use his own measures to thwart nature's
    healing process.

Sudden emotional excitements are harmful.

Medical science without diet is of little use. He is a fool
    who trusts medicine when diet can help.

Bloodletting, purging, and similar measures should be un-
    dertaken only in extreme emergency.

The face is the mirror of body and soul.

One must not injure one's neighbor.

Such is the broad framework within which Linnaeus
treated dietetics. *Lachesis naturalis* follows similar lines, although with a different arrangement and a greater emphasis
on quotations. But there also are occasional compressions
into catchword form, as well as a mixture of Swedish and
Latin, often appearing side by side in the same sentence.
Judging by its form, the work seems to have been primarily
material for a lecture series which, for the most part at least,
was not revised for publication. The students' notes of these
lectures, which have been preserved in considerable numbers, indicate that Linnaeus must have delivered thoroughly

captivating and lively discourses. The applause and merriment of the hearers show that he must have been a popular success. He himself repeatedly mentioned with pride the large number of auditors that he attracted by this particular course—so many, in fact, that members of other faculties must have attended. Linnaeus also gave private seminars in dietetics for students of theology because he wished to spread a knowledge of a healthful and natural way of life and the ability to recognize simple illnesses. The dietetics lectures were not only popular but for decades had wide influence among the Swedish people. Linnaeus's ideas were spread by his students when they left Uppsala, especially by those who became country pastors. Some reports indicate that they are current in a few areas even down to the present day.

In addition to his works on intermittent fever, Linnaeus did research on the widespread diseases of the time, and the results were presented in dissertations on leprosy (1765), scurvy (1775), ergotism (1763), and occupational ailments (1765). At that time leprosy still occurred in the northern provinces of Sweden, in Finland, on the island of Götland, and most of all in Norway. Occasionally there were isolated cases in Stockholm and Uppsala. Cases of scurvy kept occurring in large numbers. The use of sauerkraut as a remedy, introduced by the Englishman James Lind, was recommended by Linnaeus to his fellow countrymen. Ergot poisoning had broken out in great epidemics in Sweden in 1745–1746, especially in Västergötland, and in 1754–1755 in Småland and Blekinge. Linnaeus considered that this disease, known in the Middle Ages as "St. Anthony's fire," must be caused by contamination of grain through *Raphanus raphanistrum*. Thus he came very close to solving the riddle of this mysterious sickness.*

In his dissertation *Morbi artificum* [Workmen's Diseases], Linnaeus summarized what the Italian physician Bernardino

---

* The disease is the result of chronic poisoning from the fungus *Claviceps purpurea*, which occurs as a parasite on the ears of rye, especially during wet summers. The disease occurs in two forms, one characterized by dry gangrene of the limbs (*ergotismus gangraenosus*), the others by muscle spasms (*ergotismus convulsivus*).

Ramazzini, founder of the doctrine of occupational diseases, had written in his classic work *De morbis artificum* [Concerning the Diseases of Workmen] (1700). In contrast to Ramazzini, however, he provided concise and pithy descriptions of the health hazards of the various professions and added his own views and his observations in Sweden. For example, he wrote of the hazards confronting his colleagues:

> During their visits with patients, Doctors *(medici)* are often infected by epidemic illnesses such as the plague, typhus, dysentery, intermittent fever, and coughs; by bad air when they sit at sickbeds; and also by brooding (ruminating) they become melancholy.

That some illnesses are handed on from person to person, that they are contagious, was known to the doctors of antiquity. And in the seventeenth century a school of thought known as *pathologia animata* [the germ theory of disease] had developed in opposition to the concepts of the iatrophysicists and the iatrochemists.* It was based on the findings of medical microscopy, then in process of development. However, the representatives of this school not only held microorganisms responsible for the obvious contagiousness of conspicuous diseases, the extremists among them saw in microorganisms the only cause of all health disturbances. Linnaeus did not concur in this teaching; rather he adopted a critical and reserved attitude toward its most prominent champion, the Leipzig professor August Quirinus Rivinus. He did, however, suggest that microorganisms caused several illnesses which are now known to be caused by bacteria or viruses. In a paper published in the *Transactions* of the Academy of Sciences in 1750, he wrote: "It can very possibly be that smallpox, measles, dysentery, syphilis—yes, the plague itself—are caused by the smallest worms." In two dissertations that appeared later (1757, 1767), he further developed his theory of the role of the *animalcula viva* and

---

* The iatrophysicists attempted to explain all biological and pathological phenomena through physical processes. The iatrochemists attempted the same thing through chemical processes. Both schools attained their greatest influence in the seventeenth century.

included whooping cough, smallpox, intermittent fever, tuberculosis, and leprosy among the diseases caused and communicated in this way. He had earlier concluded, from the unimaginable speed of increase in these agents invisible to the naked eye, that the rapidity of reproduction in living creatures is inversely proportional to their size. He was naturally strengthened in his view by the example of the mite *(acarus)* which the Italian physician Giovanni Cosimo Bonomo first recognized and described in 1687 as the cause of scabies. Linnaeus owned a loupe microscope, which is preserved in the Linnaeus Museum in Uppsala, but to what extent his ideas were borne out by his personal investigations cannot be determined from his published works. He was convinced that the doctors of his time would in many cases have to content themselves with surmise and leave confirmation to later generations. An example of his almost prophetic penetration appears in the dissertation entitled *Mundus invisibilis* [The Invisible World]:

> It is no wonder that these microorganisms which, in respect to smallness, exceed a hundredfold the dust particles dancing in a sunbeam, can drift about in the air and be broadcast everywhere. The very smallest animals quite possibly cause greater devastations than the largest; yes, they perhaps kill more men than all the wars.

These writings on applied medicine show that in addition to his medical teaching Linnaeus engaged to some extent in actual practice in Uppsala. Although next to nothing is known about the cases he treated, two surviving accounts are of special interest. One is the earliest description of an aphasia, which was published in the *Transactions* of the Academy of Sciences in 1745. The symptoms of the Uppsala professor who suffered from this disease are so well described in a few sentences that any doctor today could make the proper diagnosis. The other case is that of a Norwegian merchant who in 1748 came to Linnaeus in Uppsala, perhaps to get advice about introducing tobacco culture into his country. The visitor suddenly fell ill, was treated by Linnaeus, but died a few days later. He had obviously been the victim of toxic diphtheria.

In no field of medicine did Linnaeus work with greater success and in a more comprehensive scientific fashion than in pharmacology. The teaching of materia medica, as the subject was called in his time, was among the duties of his professorship. He brought to its scientific development, through his great botanical knowledge and his orderly, practical method of work, completely unique qualifications. From 1738 to 1740 he was occupied with the medicaments contained in the Stockholm Pharmacopeia of 1686, which at that time was the official dispensatory, and in the medical list of 1699. He arranged the "official" medicinal plants according to his system and added instructions for the preparation of each drug for the use of druggists. This work, which was preserved in manuscript and published by the Swedish Linnean Society in 1954, also marks the beginning of his efforts to improve the current pharmacopeia. Through his friend Abraham Bäck, the president of the College of Medicine, he exercised a decisive influence on the organization of the first edition of the Swedish prescription book, which was eventually published in 1774. As early as 1749 Linnaeus in a letter to Bäck had urged a revision of the prescription book then obligatory for Swedish druggists.[5] In 1752 the College of Medicine, obviously at the instigation of Bäck, received a commission from the king to prepare a new pharmaceutical work. But the members of the College were slow in getting under way, and it was only after Bäck took over the revision in 1761 that progress was visible. The letters exchanged between Bäck and Linnaeus show how often Linnaeus was asked for advice and how much he contributed to the work. His own pharmacological writings had appeared earlier: in 1749 *Materia medica* in which medicines from vegetable sources are treated; a year later a dissertation describing medicines from the animal kingdom; and in 1752, in another dissertation, an inventory of the remedies from the mineral kingdom.

Linnaeus also discussed special questions in the field of pharmacology in a large number of dissertations, some of which refer directly to the revision of the pharmacopeia. He repeatedly pointed out the need to give preference to simple medicaments over compound ones. In *Materia medica* he goes so far as to say: "Whoever prescribes medicines with long formulas sins, either out of deceitfulness or out of ignorance."

A later edition of *Materia medica*, revised by his German pupil J. C. D. Schreber and published in Leipzig in 1772, furnishes a complete view of Linnaeus's teaching in pharmacology. Naturally Linnaeus thought that this new edition would have been even better if he had edited it himself.[6] Even in its first edition *Materia medica* had constituted an important reference work for doctors and druggists. In tabular form and with epigrammatic brevity, the medical plants, for the most part tested by Linnaeus himself, were listed, along with their alternative names, their place of origin, their pharmacological effect, the usual recommended form of application, and the preparations in which they were contained.

Linnaeus laid great stress on using native plants for medicines as far as possible, not only for reasons of economy but more importantly to guarantee freshness and to be able to test for purity. He also recommended the cultivation of special medicinal plants in southern Sweden, and in a dissertation in 1753 he proposed a list of such plants. Furthermore, he gave guidelines for the gathering, preservation, and preparation of plants, and he constantly reminded druggists of their responsibility for the purity and efficacy of their medicines.

Attempts to arrange medicinal plants and remedies in definite groups have been made since ancient times. Linnaeus's new arrangement was made according to therapeutic effectiveness. He began with the assumption that plants that have a natural relationship with one another also have similar or identical medical effects, a principle which is still accepted today. In addition, he regarded the smell and taste of plants as natural indications of their specific effectiveness. In so doing, he was asserting in the language of the time a dependence upon chemical composition. Medicines with strong odors, in his opinion, affected principally the nervous system. Altogether, his division of plants for medical use was based on ten kinds of smell and ten kinds of taste, and its purpose was to provide guidelines for recognizing what a specific medicine could do. This line of thought, so important in the history of pharmacology, has not as yet had sufficient recognition. Since these writings belong more to pharmaceutical botany, their pharmacological element has received less consideration in scientific history than it deserved. For Linnaeus himself, these publications had the practicality and usefulness of a guide for the future. On the basis of his own observations and conclusions he considered specific problems and expressed his attitude toward them. Thus the aversion of doctors to strong medicines prompted him to state that whether a substance was to be regarded as a "poison" or a "medicine" depended upon dosage, and that the exclusion of so-called poisons from the medical armamentarium was simply a sign of ignorance of the operation of medicine in general.

When Linnaeus arranged diseases in a system he wanted to make it easier to identify symptoms, and he also was looking for relationships between the individual groups of illnesses and the various classes of medicines. But in his time pathology was based almost exclusively on symptoms of illnesses, not on their causes. For this reason his efforts had no immediately fruitful results, but they deserve respect as a definite move in the direction of rational medicine, an approach that continues to be characteristic of Swedish medicine.

Linnaeus gave the title *Clavis medicinae duplex* [The Double Key to Medicine] to a work of thirty-one pages in which he sought to define the inner relationships between diagnosis and therapy, between symptoms and the effect of medicine. This book is also in the form of tables, and its content can be interpreted only with difficulty. Linnaeus said that to understand it "even the most learned would require a lifetime."[7] The human body is compared to the structure of a plant and is assumed to consist of bark *(Corticale vitale)* and core *(Medullare animale)*. The "bark" is supposed to come from the father; according to Linnaeus it consists of bones, muscles, blood, and entrails. To the "core," which comes from the mother, belong the brain and nervous system. The bark corresponds to the outer key and the core to the inner key. One would surely be right in assuming that observations in hereditary and constitutional biology led to this interpretation. Linnaeus's conception of the effect of drugs is based on the notion that the bark is affected by medicines characterized by taste and the core by those characterized by smell.

Linnaeus's first direct contact with surgery was in Uppsala in the fall of 1732. He attended a private lecture series by his fellow student Petrus Hamnerin, who had served a six-year apprenticeship under a well-known Stockholm master surgeon before taking up the study of medicine. Linnaeus's notes on these sessions have been preserved. Later, to be sure, he consistently showed distrust toward the surgeons in the exclusive and class-conscious Society of Surgeons, which under the leadership of able representatives educated abroad had emerged from the condition of barber-surgeons. To their efforts to improve the education of their successors he opposed the demand that surgery be included in the university curriculum. Thus, in a speech *De Chirugiae fundamento ex medicina* [Concerning the Medical Foundation of Surgery] in 1747, he pointed out that a thorough knowledge of general medicine and above all of anatomy was the indispensable prerequisite of any education in sugery and that this could only be offered at the universities. Over a decade later, in 1758, he urged the completion of medical students' education by having them witness operations in the university hospital. It was a special satisfaction to him when in 1775 his pupil Adolf Murray was called to the chair of anatomy and surgery; surgery finally had its own departmental representative in the University of Uppsala.

Linnaeus expressed views on other questions of medical education and measures for the public health. In so far as the College of Medicine, of which he became an honorary member in 1773, was involved in this area, his close association with Bäck again proved advantageous. He was angered by the fact that during the war in Pomerania (1757–1762) certain Swedish army surgeons, and later certain Swedish medical students, who had not fulfilled the requirements at Uppsala, received medical degrees from the medical faculty of the University of Greifswald. Political considerations, however, made it impossible for those in authority to give heed to Linnaeus's complaints.[8] He contributed to the health education of the masses as a necessary precondition for the acceptance of his dietetics by writing popular essays on such subjects as brandy and the drinking of chocolate and tea. He also wrote for the general public about the sicknesses of animals and supported the establishment of proper education for veterinarians, a subject that was entrusted to his pupil Pehr Hernquist.

But it was not only as a department head or as dean that Linnaeus dealt with medical education. He also raised his authoritative voice on general questions of curriculum and instruction. Untouched by time are the demands he expressed in 1759 in a rectorial address in the presence of the reigning king, Adolphus Frederick, and the royal family:

> If the sciences are to be brought to fruition with proper vigor it is necessary:
>
> that the sciences should be allowed to enjoy ennobling freedom,
>
> that professors should be adequately compensated so that they do not have to divide up their time to earn a living,
>
> that they should work in competition with one another and not under compulsion; for an unwilling nurse raises stepchildren,
>
> that the sciences should be as attractively presented as possible to the student, so that the latter may feel spontaneous love for them,
>
> that the young people who have made respectable progress in the sciences should receive credit and not have worked in vain.[9]

From this survey of Linnaeus's many-sided practical and experimental activity in the field of medicine, his powerful influence for the furtherance of public health, and his responsible and farsighted attitude as a university professor, it is easy to understand why he was regarded in his own country during his lifetime as a great doctor and a brilliant example of the true professor and honored accordingly. Much of his medical work, however, also deserves credit as an important contribution to the general development of medicine.

11

Traveler and Ethnologist

The reports Linnaeus wrote about his journeys through several Swedish provinces belong today to the classic works of Swedish literature. They mark the beginning of the "discovery of Sweden," in the scientific sense of an investigation into folklore, economics, geography, and plant and animal life. Along with the wonders of nature, however, Linnaeus paid attention to historic structures, ancient cult sites, evidences of older cultures, and historic episodes preserved by oral tradition. He reveals himself in these writings as few men who are remembered for their scientific achievements have done. The reports show him as a man of his own time, seeing and experiencing nature and people in his homeland. It is not surprising that even today new editions continue to appear regularly in Sweden and are widely read.

Chronologically his travels fall into two groups, the trips to Lapland, Bergslagen, and Dalecarlia in the period before his trip to Holland, and the three long journeys through Öland and Gotland, Västergötland and Skäne in the 1740s. A study of the account of these two sets of journeys reveals clear internal evidence of the difference between them. The manuscripts of the earlier explorations were not published until the nineteenth century, but the reports of the later journeys came out in book form a few years after the expeditions, two of them in German translation as well.

It is probable that Linnaeus did not hit upon the idea of these inland journeys all by himself. However, during his brief stay in Lund he went on natural-history excursions of varying lengths in the environs of the city, and it is perfectly conceivable that he was already considering trips to other sections of his native land. In 1729—that is, barely a year after Linnaeus's departure for Uppsala—his teacher Kilian Stobaeus worked out a list of instructions for an exploratory journey through Skåne. Stobaeus could not make the trip because of his physical infirmity and he wanted his pupils to have guidelines for their observations. The text of this travel guide was among the writings left by Linnaeus; because of its subject matter and the time it was written, it is fair to assume that Linnaeus had Stobaeus to thank for his comprehensive program of observation and investigation. Beyond question, however, Linnaeus himself had special qualifications for just such ethnological investigations, since, as the son of a country parson, he had close connections with the peasant population, whose daily life in eighteenth-century Sweden did not essentially differ from that of a pastor's house.

On the later journeys he was, as the reports clearly indicate, very deeply concerned with the economic point of view. Early in 1741 the Imperial Diet had decreed that Linnaeus should carry out journeys "to Gotland, Öland, and other places in order to gain information about grasses suitable for dyes and other useful plants." The journeys to Västergötland and Skåne were also commissioned by the government. There is no doubt, however, that the suggestions came either directly or indirectly from Linnaeus himself. The usefulness of science to the state so imbued the spirit of the times that in fact it played a decisive role in the founding of the Academy of Sciences. Sweden owes to Linnaeus the fact that more attention has been paid there than in other countries to the economic uses of natural science. Beyond this, however, in perpetuation of his memory, the Swedish people have retained and cultivated, up to the present day and in spite of occasional countercurrents, his love of nature and of his native landscape. Only those who have visited Sweden and seen the profound feeling for nature and tradition, the universal participation each year in the earliest signs of approaching spring, the sense of personal relationship to one's own province, and the overt treasuring of the homeland, can appreciate the full extent of Linnaeus's life work. Thus do the inhabitants of Sweden continue, though often unconsciously, the traditions of their great countryman.

His first trip, which took him to Lapland, involved considerable personal danger. In his report of his adventures Linnaeus shows himself to have been an enterprising man who made his way through vast unknown regions with youthful ardor and not without a certain taste for the sensational. One trait of the true explorer is missing—the stubborn pursuit of a geographical goal. Linnaeus's principal interest was the plant world of Lapland; therefore *Flora Lapponica* was the chief result of his journey. His study of the customs of the nomadic Lapps had, as mentioned before, considerable bearing on his teaching of dietetics, and it later led to comparisons with habits and usages in other Swedish provinces. After his return from Lapland he ordered a Lapp costume, which he took with him to Holland and wore in Hartekamp when he posed for the 1737 portrait by Martin Hoffmann. His reports of the journeys to Dalecarlia, 1733 and 1734, contain, in addition to the completely realistic account of his descent into the mine in Falun, detailed explanations of mining techniques there and mineralogical observations.

The reader who encounters these travel journals for the first time cannot fail to be impressed by the succinct, striking descriptions and the clear arrangement of the material. The form—a day by day record—makes for ease in looking up individual observations and unquestionably is another expression of Linnaeus's passion for order, which shows itself elsewhere in his literary works by the inclusion of tables. The vividness of his portrayals of nature is best illustrated by quotation. Apropos of the journey from Västergötland to Uppsala, Linnaeus gives us in a few sentences a picture of the autumn landscape in Närke province:

From Fallingsbrö onward, autumn was constantly before our eyes; the forest, to be sure, still retained its green, but a deeper and soberer green than in summer. Pastures and meadows were green as well but without flowers, which cattle had devoured in the former and the scythe shorn away in the latter. The fields were yellow with stubble and ornamented with green weeds. The ditches were full of water because of the wet summer, and a multitude of *Bidens tripartita* gave them a yellow color. The sides of the road were covered with waterpepper *(Polygonum hydropiper)* which was beginning to turn red and droop its ears. Farmers everywhere were busy in the fields, some mowing the grain with scythes, while their womenfolk, strikingly white in face and hands, tied it up; some loading it, some threshing, some grinding the grain, some smoothing the field with iron harrows, some sowing winter rye, some plowing barley under, some dragging rollers; meanwhile the shepherd boys were singing beside their flocks and blowing their horns, as the flocks grazed on the mowed fields, until the evening air grew more penetrating and the sun sank beneath the horizon at the time of our return to the garden in Uppsala.[1]

When Linnaeus is describing plants and animals he pays strict attention to essentials.

The leaves of the hornbeam in the hedges were almost without exception rolled up, with the edges bent inward so that the under side was convex and the raised vessels of the leaf had become very crinkled. We surmised that they had been rolled up by plant lice, but did not find a single one, therefore we could not decide whether the severe drought in the spring had been the cause or whether this was a new species with curled leaves.[2]

Toads, *Rana bufo*, love shadowy places, especially at the foot of mountains, where the foul-smelling *Stachys* and the *Actea spicata* grow. I do not know why these ugly creatures take such great delight in these fetid plants; I have seen toads creep into a house when *Stachys foetida* has been taken indoors; in the Ukraine where the foul-smelling camomiles, *Anthemis cotula*, grows more profusely than elsewhere, there are so many toads that all the houses are full of them and as soon as the former are thrown out the toads disappear as well. I set a dog after a big toad, he bit it, but then shook his head very wildly, showing thereby that his curiosity had done him harm, nor could he be provoked afterwards to a new attack; and so what Lister reports is credible, that if one takes hold of this creature with tongs, harmful or poisonous juice squirts out of each wart.[3]

In all his travel journals, and especially in the one about his trip to Skåne, Linnaeus was at pains to describe agricultural conditions, plants and their cultivation, animal husbandry, and pest control, as well as a great variety of technical agricultural matters. His critical attitude and naturalist's sharp eye are evident, and so is his wish to acquire experience and pass it on in the public interest. His desire that his knowledge should be useful to men is as evident as are his curiosity and his constant passion for learning about the unknown, the still hidden.

For the most part, beech trees are trimmed up above and topped, for when the dweller in the plains goes to get firewood he climbs into the tree and strikes off the crown, which can be more easily packed into a wagonload and requires less strength to chop up. For this reason fewer trees are missing, but the beech tree suffers more from being topped than do other trees.[4]

Beehives were not to be seen in this countryside, whereas they had been so numerous in Öland. Here there was no heath: this would mean that the honey would be lighter in color if bees were introduced here. To be sure, we were told that the late Bishop Esberg had brought bees here earlier, but the fact that they finally disappeared should not be thought prejudicial since he lived in Visby where they were exposed to the daily wind and the swarms had their best chance for protection in the many old churches and towers.[5]

Bedbugs are disposed of by many methods; however, I have heard none praised with so much confidence as the following: the walls of the room are coated with turpentine which is then ignited with a candle; then the flame shoots up quickly and kills the bugs. But one must have water at hand, although this flame does not easily cause a fire. Those who wish to experiment with this must remember what Hippocrates said: *experimentum est periculosum* [experimentation is perilous], especially if one is confronting an old worm-eaten wall, its crannies stuffed with moss. Others report a safer method, namely *Mentha sylvestris* [wild mint], which is said to kill the bugs instantly.[6]

To Linnaeus as a dietician, the health of the population was of special interest. He tried to track down the reasons for the presence or absence of many diseases in order to find the means of prevention and to recognize the causes. With what sensitive and almost loving consideration he regarded the customs of his fellow countrymen is shown in this small observation from his youthful trip to Dalecarlia:

The local parson said that in this neighborhood there are many old people and almost a hundred that have lived their seventy years. One old woman is said to be living in Björbo who is 105 years old and is still fairly strong. There is nothing to be observed about the inhabitants that is especially serviceable to the maintenance of good health except that in this region they are more than elsewhere quite modest and cheerful.[7]

In the same report, severe pulmonary disease among the stone grinders caused by the dust is so well described by Linnaeus that a knowledgeable doctor today can easily recognize the symptoms. Especially noteworthy is the emphasis he places on the social fate of these invalids and his conclusions about the absence of contagion among the families.

It must not be forgotten that these sick people have come to their miserable condition thinking that they were supporting their lives, when they were rather destroying them. All those who earn a living in the grinding mills seldom reach a greater age than twenty, thirty, or at most forty years. (From this one can judge the condition of the widows, the minor children, and the household.) For the stone dust, although the greater part of it is drawn off through the chimney, nevertheless is breathed constantly in large amounts into the lungs, into the bronchial tubes and into the cells of the lungs, where it is held fast by the mucous and fluid with which it is continuously moistened; because of warmth it adheres, and since it cannot free itself grows into nodules that obstruct the vescicles of the lungs, from which ulcers result and true phthisis. When anyone develops a rattling in the throat and his shoulders shake, people quickly conclude that he already has the lime in his body, on account of which he will enter into the silence. Moreover, they themselves believe that their fate is not determined so much by the stone dust as by the water they drink during their working time which has stood in the quarry and has picked up harmful particles. Even more in the fall if they drink the water when they are hot and sweating. In church a few old men were to be seen, but we were told that their professions were that of tailor and shoemaker and not laborers in the quarry. Noteworthy too is the fact that their wives and children are free from consumption, although phthisis is considered to be an inheritable and contagious disease.[8]

Linnaeus and his traveling companions looked up a local quack in Västergötland, tested his abilities, and revealed his ignorance. This quack was typical of a group of healers who were still operating in large sections of Europe in the eighteenth century. Indeed to this very day frauds of the sort of "Sven in Bragnum" are to be found, defying all the advances of medical science and harmless to those who, also in ignorance, let themselves be successfully treated.

There were three very famous quacks in Västergötland, namely: the old man in Enekulle, Sven in Bragnum, and his pupil Waltin Sträng in the Kinnewald parish. People went to consult them about their diseases just as though they were the best doctors. Since we were only a quarter of a mile from the home of Sven in Bragnum we went there to hear his wisdom.

Sven in Bragnum had bought a small house in which he had arranged a little dark room as a dispensary. He was a farmhand some thirty-odd years old, but his hair was already beginning to turn gray and his sedentary way of life had endowed him with considerable corpulence. When we came to him and greeted him, he stood motionless without touching his hat or troubling us with any ceremonies. He was free in conversation but serious. My companions could not restrain themselves from pretending to sicknesses in order to get his advice. One of them, Herr T., said that he had been spitting blood; Sven inquired about his home and his way of life and advised him to buy powder for the blood-spitting in an apothecary shop in Göteborg; he asked too whether the patient had been bled, but the latter said no and that he was afraid of it, but he was given the advice to be bled in the arm. The other, Herr L., asked for a remedy against roaring in the ears; the fellow replied that he should not use any remedy since the more he consumed the worse it would be, he should only have a vein under the lobe of his ear opened in the place where there were three veins, of which the middle one must be chosen; however, he could also heat a silver spoon, pour some spirits of wine into it and allow the vapor to be drawn into his ear. The patient asked what had caused the illness. The fellow replied that it was blood that had dripped into the outer ear. The patient pretended that the roaring had moved from one ear to the other and asked whether the two ears were connected. This was answered affirmatively. One of my companions asked to talk privately to the fellow; they both went into a room apart and the patient pretended that he had followed evil courses and had contracted a venereal flux; the fellow promised to cure him, gave him a coarse vegetable powder which cost 16 Stüber to take with brandy and white of egg; the patient went on to ask what sort of diet he should follow. The fellow said it didn't matter provided he ate nothing for an hour before taking the medicine. The patient asked whether he might drink brandy too. The fellow replied that it should be taken in brandy. The patient went on to say that he was accustomed to three draughts of brandy a day, whereupon the other remarked that this amounted to nothing at all. We had brought hemlock along with us, which caused the fellow to ask what we intended to do with the *Angelica* [wild carrot]. We replied that we had found it near Trimstorp and that it was poisonous. The fellow shook his head and laughed at us, saying that it was neither harmful nor beneficial but that he would eat it all up, and with this intention tried to take some of it, which I would not permit.[9]

The great interest in Linnaeus's travel journals in Sweden today can be properly understood only if one takes into account the many descriptions of cities, towns, country residences and parsonages, sometimes very brief, but on occasion in full detail and in every case written with great vividness. A good example is the description of his impressions of Göteborg on his trip through Västergötland in 1746:

Göteborg is the most beautiful city in the whole kingdom, in size somewhat smaller than Uppsala, almost exactly circular, defended by walls and moats, with regular, straight, level streets intersected by various canals on both sides of which there are sidewalks. The walled sides of the canals are made of fieldstone so that the streets are at a man's height above the water; the bridges over the canals are vaulted and both sides are lined with trees so that this city looks very much like the Dutch cities. The buildings are for the most part big and strong but of wood, two stories high, built close together, faced on the outside with boards and painted red or yellow with white or blue trim and window casements. At a distance they look like stone buildings, the foundation walls are also faced with boards. They are roofed with slate and the windows are of English or French glass. The *Gothic Elbe* [Göta Alv river] flows close by the city and is joined to it by canals; but on the western side a bay of the sea extends up to the city so that large ships can come within a mile or half a mile of the city and find a safe harbor there; little craft however can come right into the city. In other directions the city is separated from the sea by a pair of high mountains. It lies rather low so that many houses have to be built on piles; as a result the water in the canals often becomes rather foul-smelling and hence the place is not very healthy. In this city is the residence of the governor, a secondary school, a handsome town hall and exchange, the Admiralty, the Armory, a garrison, three churches, two burgomasters, and the East India Company. The convenient ship route from the great western ocean without the necessity of passing through the sound greatly simplifies commerce and hence most of the citizens devote themselves to trade and shipping. The city is crowded with merchants, seamen, yeomanry, strangers, and people who stream in from the whole country; therefore there is much wealth among the inhabitants and one finds beautifully and elaborately furnished houses.

The castles, the Gothic Lion [Göta Leijon] in the northeast and the Crown [Kronan] in the south, stand on separate hills, are squat, cylindrical with rectangular foundations, and are provided with firing ports on all sides.[10]

These examples of Linnaeus's work as a travel writer indicate the wealth of observation and the unique quality of his reporting, as well as the personality traits that are reflected in it. Even though this part of his literary work has already been frequently examined from various scientific points of view, a reading of the original conveys such an impressive picture of eighteenth-century Sweden that its worth would not be diminished if it were considered without reference to the identity of the author.

12

Friends and Foes

During his lifetime Linnaeus was honored and admired in his homeland. To be sure, he had opponents, and there were those who envied him, yet the greater his foreign reputation became, the more attention was paid to his work by his fellow countrymen. Among his friends two were especially close to him, Carl Gustaf Tessin and Abraham Bäck. The large role that both played in his life has already been made clear.

Tessin, benefactor of his country as promoter of science and the arts and unquestionably Linnaeus's most influential patron, also had a genuine love for the natural sciences. He openly admired Linnaeus as the leading scholar in Sweden. Linnaeus publicly recorded his thanks with the dedication of his most important works, beginning with the second edition of *Systema naturae*. Their friendship endured for three decades.

On a different level entirely were his relations with Abraham Bäck, whom he loved like his own brother, as is evident from the many surviving letters. Linnaeus shared with Bäck wholly personal concerns and greatly valued his advice. Whenever he went to Stockholm he stayed in Bäck's house, and Bäck was repeatedly Linnaeus's guest in Uppsala and Hammarby. The exchange of ideas between these two men, who were so important in the intellectual and medical spheres of their time, was not confined to science. Their letters also dealt with university matters, with general politics, and often with highly confidential personal affairs. The inner worth of this scholarly friendship is revealed not only through its intellectual wealth but in its genuine human warmth and familiar directness.

In Sweden there was no real scientific opposition to Linnaeus, if one excepts the feud with Wallerius in 1741 and the long rivalry with Rosén which toward the end of the rivals' lives was resolved into friendship. Linnaeus's unchallenged position in his own country is not really surprising, for the favor of the royal house and of important dignitaries had raised him and his work above open controversy.

It was otherwise abroad, where scholars were divided into two camps according to their view of the sexual system of plant classification. Many who were in agreement with its principles of organization and recognized the necessity of an artificial system nevertheless took offense at one or another minor point. Linnaeus's autocratic procedure in the matter of nomenclature, for instance, was held against him.

Special attention has been paid to his relations with Albrecht von Haller. The acquaintance was begun in 1737 by Linnaeus who took the publication of Haller's *Dissertatio de methodo studii botanici absque praeceptore* [Botany Self-Taught] as an occasion for writing to its author. The scientific correspondence thus begun continued for twelve years. The two men never met and so the written word remained their only method of communicating with each other. Very likely this contributed to a situation where misunderstandings and small disagreements led finally to a break. At first, however, the correspondence was a lively exchange of news about medicine and botany, about books and academic writings, as well as personal matters. Haller reviewed the Swedish works sent to him in his *Göttinger gelehrte Anzeigen* [Göttinger Scholastic Notices] and thereby contributed substantially to their acceptance in the scholarly world. To be sure, even though the correspondence was most friendly in tone, there was never any agreement between the two on important botanical questions, for Haller rejected the sexual system and demanded a natural method of classifying plants. Moreover, he joined those who sharply criticized Linnaeus's high-handedness in working out his nomenclature. To the binomial nomenclature as such he had no objection, but Linnaeus's replacement of familiar plant names with his own inventions went against Haller's desire to preserve scientific traditions. Yet each acknowledged the scientific talents of the other, even in the realm of botany. In 1739, when Haller first seriously thought of returning to Switzerland, he considered the matter of Linnaeus's becoming his successor in the Göttingen professorship. Until 1745 their relations remained untroubled, at least outwardly. But in that year, when Linnaeus in *Flora Suecia* came out openly against Haller's botanical views, a strong rejoinder came from Göttingen. Haller in his review made himself very clear: "In various places certain expressions and refutations have slipped from the author's pen, the rashness of which would be easy to refute if we were either willing to engage in polemics or did not, with a certain humanity, hold Herr L.'s other merits to his credit."

Enraged because he was the only person to receive unfavorable comment in this book and because all but one of the plant names he had introduced had been changed, Haller was not reconciled by soothing letters and alterations in the text of the new edition. Linnaeus on his side now became distrustful, suspecting Haller of intrigues and imputing to his influence the attacks of other German scholars. The ending of the correspondence in the fall of 1749 was certainly connected with the appearance in Göttingen of five polemical articles against Linnaeus's botanical views, under the name of Haller's sixteen-year-old son, Gottlieb Emanuel. Linnaeus had no doubt that the father was speaking through the son, and presently this was proved by young Haller's asking his forgiveness.

Some years later (1754), after Haller had finally left Göttingen, the curator of Göttingen University, Gerlach Adolf Baron von Münchhausen, inquired of Linnaeus whether he would be willing to take over Haller's chair. A letter to Bäck shows the optimism that Linnaeus felt at the very thought of this assignment: "Believe me, I would draw half the youth of Germany to Göttingen through natural history."[1] But the ties with his native land and the University of Uppsala proved too strong and he remained in Sweden. He was filled with satisfaction, however, when his most gifted and devoted pupil, Johann Andreas Murray, became professor of medicine and botany in Göttingen in 1764.

Twice later Linnaeus made attempts to resume relations with Haller. In March 1766 he wrote him a letter and sent him a copy of *Clavis medicinae,* which he had dedicated, among others, to Haller as *physiologo summo* [greatest physiologist]. But Haller's letter of acknowledgment did not open the way to a renewed correspondence. One of Haller's letters to the Swiss mathematician and botanist Johann Gesner indicates that in 1772 Linnaeus, through Johann Andreas Murray, made a further attempt at reconciliation, also in vain.

Haller has been described as irreconcilable toward others in controversy. He has been justly criticized for publishing in 1773–1774 a selection of letters addressed to him without previously informing the writers. Letters from Linnaeus were among them, printed not only without his consent and without deleting completely private communications but also with the Latin grammatical and orthographical mistakes uncorrected. (The story that Linnaeus's rage at this caused his first stroke has been disproved.) But in a few cases malice has been imputed to Haller where mere carelessness was to blame.

There seems to be no doubt that Linnaeus felt truly disturbed by his quarrel with Haller. In Haller's eyes, however, Linnaeus continued to be the man who "had thrown the whole of botany into confusion."[2] Understandably enough, this scholarly dispute aroused great interest, what with the prominence of both men in the scientific life of their century and the long-lasting influence of their lives, whose spans coincided almost to the year.

Other botanists also expressed more or less serious doubts about the sexual system and Linnaeus's procedure in the matter of nomenclature. Among his scientific opponents were Johann Jakob Dillenius, who came from Darmstadt and had been professor of botany at Oxford since 1728; Lorenz Heister, Helmstedt professor of medicine and botany, who was famous principally for his pioneering work as a surgeon; Johann Georg Siegesbeck in St. Petersburg; and Christian Gottlieb Ludwig in Leipzig. The dispute with Heister caused Linnaeus the greatest concern. Unquestionably Heister was a gifted botanist; he had protested loudly against Linnaeus's nomenclature and had proposed a system of classification of plants of his own according to the characteristics of their leaves. In letters and articles he engaged vigorously in the battle of opinions. Linnaeus answered these attacks by gradually eliminating Heister's name from the later editions of his botanical works. Behind Siegesbeck's attacks Linnaeus suspected for a time the influence of Haller, but even more that of Heister. Siegesbeck, who had been superintendent of the botanical gardens in St. Petersburg since 1735, had formerly been a teacher of physics in Helmstedt and was indebted to Heister for the successful recommendation to his new post. In this controversy with Siegesbeck an ally for Linnaeus appeared in the person of Dr. Johann Gottlieb Gleditsch, known as a botanist and superintendent of the Botanical Gardens in Berlin. By fertilizing a female palm, *Chamaerops humilis* L., in his garden with pollen of the same species which he had received from the botanical garden in Leipzig, Gleditsch had presented a successful proof of sexuality in the plant kingdom. This test, known as the *experimentum Berolinense*, made a great impression because of the simplicity of its execution.

Linnaeus dreaded public quarrels with his scientific opponents. The continuation of his systematic work was in his eyes the most effective rejoinder. For this reason others were all the more ready to step in on his behalf. Often, as with Gleditsch, these were scholars who knew him only from his writings or with whom he had corresponded. The strongest support, however, came from his own pupils. Those of his students who under his instructions undertook expeditions to faraway lands in order to gather unknown plants, animals, and minerals and to carry out studies of national customs are discussed later. Among his Swedish pupils Johann Andreas Murray played an outstanding role as mediator, especially in respect to Linnaeus's influence in the German-speaking world.

Murray, the son of a pastor of the German community in Stockholm, grew up bilingual. An older stepbrother had become professor of philosophy in Göttingen in 1755, establishing relations for the whole family with this influential center of intellectual life. His younger brother, Adolf Murray, was named professor of anatomy and surgery in Uppsala in 1774. Johann Andreas Murray went to Göttingen in 1760, three years later was named reader in botany, in the following year assistant professor, and in 1769 full professor of medicine and botany. In connection with the latter appointment he promised Linnaeus in a letter "by word and deed to spread and defend the flawless achievements of his great teacher."[3] In his reply Linnaeus wrote: "What greater satisfaction could there be for me than to see my former comrades spreading over Europe and becoming the generals in command of Flora's Army?[4] As translator of the Swedish Academy's *Transactions* in medicine and botany, Johann Andreas Murray performed great services for the scientific relations between Sweden and the continent. His *Practical Medical Library*, which appeared in three volumes between 1774 and 1781, is a mine of scientific and personal information about natural science and medicine in Sweden. When Murray visited his old teacher in Uppsala in 1772 he saw the manuscript of the considerably enlarged botanical part of *Systema naturae* and offered to find a publisher for it in Germany. His efforts were successful and two years later the *Systema vegetabilium* was published by Dietrich in Göttingen as part of the thirteenth editon of the complete work.

The Göttingen professor Johann Beckmann, whose report of his meeting with Linnaeus has already been mentioned, also came forward as a defender and parried the attacks of the Mannheim doctor and botanist Friedrich Kasimir Medicus. In this particular scholarly battle Linnaeus's lack of contact with the scientific literature of continental Europe was at the root of the trouble; his linguistic misunderstandings were often the cause of his unreasonable attitude toward many of his colleagues.

Among the German pupils, Johann Christian Daniel Schreber had corresponded with Linnaeus since 1758, in 1760 spent a half year in Uppsala, where he received his doctorate and distinguished himself by editing the reports of Linnaeus's journeys to Öland, Gotland, and Västergötland, as well as the four editions of *Materia medica* (1772–1787). The Hamburg doctor Paul Dietrich Gieseke was with Linnaeus in Uppsala in 1771; he reported on his stay in 1792 and from his description it is plain how much Linnaeus in his later years was interested in a natural classification of the plant kingdom. Gieseke in his work also made use of the lecture notes of Johann Christian Fabricius, who from 1762 to 1764 had been one of Linnaeus's auditors. In 1768 Fabricius was made professor of economy in Copenhagen and from 1775 to 1808 had the chair of economics, natural history, and public affairs at the University of Kiel. He became famous principally through his entomological works. He wrote a biographical essay on Linnaeus which was published in 1780. One of Linnaeus's supporters, though critical at times, was the Swiss Friedrich Ehrhardt, who worked in Hanover as a chemist's dispenser, went from there to Sweden in 1771, and became a pupil of Carl Wilhelm Scheele, Torbern Bergman, and Linnaeus. Upon his return he was made superintendent of the gardens at Herrenhausen. For all his admiration he was no blind adherent of Linnaeus. This clear-sighted and inventive botanist who made great contributions to our knowledge of cryptogams and grasses was a true empiricist. From him comes the warning: "Whoever wants to look upon everything Linnaeus wrote, and often altered when he had attained greater insight, as the word of God and wants to follow it blindly, let him do so; I have nothing against it, but I wish him luck."[5] In 1790 Ehrhardt published his notes on botanical excursions in the neighborhood of Uppsala.

A sharp attack on Linnaeus came from the French doctor and philosopher of materialism Julien Offray de la Mettrie, a pupil of Boerhaave. From 1748 until his death in 1751 de la Mettrie lived in Berlin as reader to Frederick the Great. He derived the inspiration for his work *L'homme plante* [The Human Plant], which appeared in Potsdam in 1748, from Linnaeus's *Classes plantarum,* but in a satirical work, *Ouvrage de Pénélope, ou le Machiavel en médecine* [Penelope's Handiwork, or Machiavelli in Medicine], which appeared in two volumes in Berlin that same year, he held up his teachers Boerhaave, Linnaeus, Artedi, and others to derision.

Linnaeus himself wrote a great deal about his relations with friends, colleagues, and pupils. An interesting sixteen-page pamphlet in octavo format, intitled *Orbis eruditi judicium de Caroli Linnaei scriptis* [The Judgment of the Learned World on the Writings of Carolus Linnaeus] which appeared in Stockholm in 1741, is a record in tabular form of the works Linnaeus published between 1735 and 1740, the opinions of foreign scholars about him, and reviews of his writings. Published at the time of the debate about Linnaeus's appointment to Lars Roberg's chair, the pamphlet was obviously designed to advertise to his patrons and friends his accomplishments and his reputation abroad. There can really be no doubt that Linnaeus himself was the author. This work became rare even in his lifetime, and after his death more copies of it were found among his papers than could be located anywhere else. Among those whose favorable opinion of Linnaeus's scientific work is cited are Boerhaave, de Gorter, Burmann, Gronovius, Sloane, Lawson, Sauvages, Jussieu, Haller, Johann Gesner, Gleditsch, and Kohl.

That not all of these remained his friends, that he had bitter opponents, and that many scientists simply could not entirely follow the later development of his thought doubtless had objective causes. One is surprised again and again, however, at how strongly subjective some of these disputes were, how personal traits and foibles played a decisive role. Linnaeus's differences with Haller clearly show how hard it was in those quarrelsome times for two men of similar interests and character to remain on friendly terms if there was a bone of contention between them from the beginning of their acquaintance.

Goethe alone formed his judgment solely from Linnaeus's writings, uninfluenced by personal considerations.[6] Himself a naturalist and a nature lover, in his younger years he had taken with him on his excursions *Philosophia botanica* and other works by Linnaeus and had studied them and he remained a devoted admirer. In a letter to the German composer Carl Friedrich Zelter on November 7, 1816, he made clear in a few words the influence of the Swedish scholar on his own thinking: "During these days I have reread Linnaeus and am startled by this extraordinary man. I have learned an enormous amount from him, not only botany. Aside from Shakespeare and Spinoza I would not know of any of the departed who has had such an influence on me."

13

Concerning the "Apostles"

It was in the year 1750 that Linnaeus for the first time designated his traveling pupils as his "apostles"; he chose the term to indicate that their task was a missionary one. Their assignment was to travel all over the world, scrutinizing nature at his direction and according to his ideas, and at the same time spreading his fame. Linnaeus was brilliantly adept at arousing enthusiasm in his hearers. At his instigation these young Swedes exposed themselves to dangers and privations in order to observe and collect in foreign lands according to the principles established by their master during his own student journeys in his native land. These travels are so indissolubly connected with Linnaeus's work and have contributed so substantially to its acceptance by the world that it is proper to consider the most important of the apostles and their travels a part of Linnaeus's life accomplishment.

The magnitude of the task can be grasped by considering that in the eighteenth century only a bare fifth of the earth's surface had been explored and something like one tenth of its plants and animals discovered. A glance at the maps of that time gives some idea of the preponderance of unexplored space in the period before the rise of colonialism. The traveling naturalist could still have the experience, hardly comprehensible today, of coming upon a land with wholly unknown flora.

Personal courage and dedication were indispensable prerequisites for men who made the exploration of nature their business. Whether the impulse to do this springs from folly or from reason was a question that Linnaeus himself raised.[1] For many, this impulse has led to early death, and among these martyrs were some of Linnaeus's pupils. Christopher Tärnström died of a tropical fever in an Indian port on his way to China, Pehr Forsskål of malaria in Yemen. Friedrich Hasselquist fell ill on his journey through Asia Minor and died near Smyrna at the age of thirty. Pehr Löfling perished in the tropics on a South American expedition, and the thirty-four-year-old Johann Peter Falck, unable to cope with the hardships of his journey through Turkestan and Mongolia, went into a depression and took his own life in Kazan. Buoyed up by youthful enthusiasm, they went out and sacrificed their lives for the science Linnaeus had taught them, and for Linnaeus too.

To their teacher it was painful to lose these promising and gallant men, many of whom rued the day they had been enticed by distant lands, and he also had to submit to reproaches. "Tärnström's death disturbs me greatly, his wife raises complaints to high heaven against me, that I lured her husband away from her and made her a helpless widow," he wrote in a letter to Bäck.[2] Hasselquist, shortly before his death, reportedly cursed the teacher who had started him on the career of naturalist.

It was due to the support of Count Tessin that Linnaeus was able to send so many apostles into foreign countries. Recommendations from Tessin to the Swedish East India Company in Göteborg resulted in young naturalists' being given free passage in sailing vessels to the Far East. The manager of that successful trading company, commercial counselor Magnus Lagerström, was a variously gifted and remarkably cultivated merchant prince. He exerted himself to fulfill every conceivable wish of Linnaeus. The ships' captains were given instructions to be helpful to the young natu-

ralists in every respect, even financially, and to aid in secur-
ing specimens. The first of Linnaeus's pupils to take ship with
the East India Company was Tarnström in 1745. He did not
reach his goal, but others were able to return home with
interesting finds and valuable observations.

Of special importance in Linnaeus's eyes was the journey
of investigation to North America made by his pupil Pehr
Kalm, who had already made trips in 1742 through Västergötland and Bohuslän and two years later through Russia
and the Ukraine, received a traveling stipend through the
efforts of his teacher. Leaving Göteberg in December 1747,
he went first to England and in August of the following year
crossed to North America. He began his investigations in the
lower part of the Delaware valley where from 1638 to 1655
a Swedish colony had been settled and a considerable number of Swedish-speaking residents still lived. In the following
year he traveled through large portions of Pennsylvania,
New Jersey, and New York, then visited the parts of Canada
settled by Europeans in several journeys lasting until early in
1751. His detailed travel reports were published shortly
thereafter, first in Swedish and then in a German translation.
They reveal his alertness for everything important to natural
history and medicine and contain interesting ethnological
and sociological observations. His contribution to botany was
especially great. Linnaeus, who had become uneasy and an-
gry because letters from his pupil were so rare, found his
return so exciting that he was led to forget an attack of gout;
"through joy at the plants, he no longer felt his illness"[3]; he
awaited his apostle's return "like a bride at one o'clock in the
morning."[4] Kalm's journey greatly enriched Linnaeus's
knowledge of the plants of North America. In *Hortus Cliffortianus* Linnaeus could mention 170 North American species.
With the help of Gronovius, whose *Flora Virginica*, 1739,
was the first book on North American flora, Linnaeus corresponded with doctors in America who were interested in
botany and received much new material from them. Kalm,
who was the first to examine systematically the regions of
North America in which he traveled, was able to discover
many new plants and turn them over to his teacher for incor-

poration in his system. *Species plantarum* finally contained more than 700 North American species, of which 90 are recorded as having been discovered by Kalm.

In 1750 Pehr Osbeck, who had distinguished himself in botany and zoology in addition to his theological studies, traveled to China as ship's chaplain for the East India Company. He brought back from his three-year journey valuable specimens and published a detailed travel journal.

In 1750 the Spanish ambassador in Stockholm, on orders from his king, proposed to Linnaeus that a capable young botanist from his school investigate the plants of Spain. This distinguished assignment fell to young Pehr Löfling, and the Academy of Sciences gave its support to the project by providing instruments. In the following year Löfling embarked on his journey; through letters he kept Linnaeus informed and sent seeds and plants to Uppsala. In 1754 the Spanish government dispatched him to South America with an expedition that was to settle a border dispute between Venezuela and Colombia and at the same time study national customs. Löfling's investigations of the plants in that area were terminated by his death only a year and a half later. Linnaeus mourned him as he would have a son. He published Löfling's travel journal in 1758 and in a foreword commemorated the achievements of this gifted and loyal apostle.

Daniel Solander, at one time favored by Linnaeus as his successor and even as a son-in-law, on his teacher's advice went to England on an assignment in 1759. In 1762 differences of opinion between the two men over a summons to St. Petersburg, which Linnaeus wanted Solander to accept, led to a breach. Later, Solander, together with the British naturalist Joseph Banks, accompanied James Cook on his first circumnavigation of the world (1768–1771). When he returned he settled permanently in England as librarian at the British Museum; his teacher never saw him again.

Pehr Forsskål was conspicuous among Linnaeus's pupils as a versatile scholar and also for his philosophical works. After undergraduate work in Uppsala he went for several years to the University of Göttingen. In 1761 he joined an expedition to the Near East outfitted by the king of Denmark. Whether

Linnaeus recommended him or connections in Göttingen led to the assignment is not altogether clear. From the beginning the expedition was ill-starred. Quarrels broke out among the participants, becoming more and more heated during the voyage through the Mediterranean from Marseilles to Alexandria and Constantinople. Forsskål, however, let nothing disturb his scientific zeal. He succeeded in overcoming the Arabs' distrust of every form of scientific collecting, which at first had hindered him, and at times even secured their assistance. The expedition proceeded by ship as far as the southern part of the Arabian peninsula and was to return by land. Though the collections and manuscript of the expedition were sent back to Europe by sea, much of the material was lost. Out of the entire expedition, only one member, reached home—the German, Karsten Niebuhr, who reappeared after seven years. It is thanks to him alone that this large-scale undertaking had any results at all. Niebuhr put together whatever had been rescued of Forsskål's notes and gave the fragments of his work to the printer, among them the important *Flora Aegyptiaco-Arabica* [Egyptian-Arabian Flora].

The most productive of the travels subsidized by the Swedish East India Company were unquestionably those of Anders Sparrmann who traveled to China in 1765 and spent two years, there, bringing back rich collections. In 1772 Sparrmann once more took ship with the East India Company, this time to South Africa, where he explored Cape Colony and joined Cook on his second expedition to Antarctica (1772-1776), in which the German botanists Johann Reinhold Forster and his son Johann Georg also took part. In 1787 Sparrmann engaged in another Swedish expedition to Africa. This was commissioned by the crown to find a suitable site on the African coast for a Swedish colony but had no success. In 1790 Sparrmann became professor of natural history and pharmacy in Stockholm and assistant in the medical college. He remained active in Stockholm as a charity doctor into old age.

Only one of Linnaeus's pupils outdid Sparrmann's achievements abroad. This was Carl Peter Thunberg, who has been called, probably with good reason, the most important naturalist in the period directly after Linnaeus. His success is attested not only by the facts of his career but by a reputation which still flourishes in the countries where he was principally active—South Africa and Japan. Thunberg was born in Jönköping in 1743 and attended secondary school there. In 1761 he went to Uppsala, soon joined the circle of students around Linnaeus, and finally took his M.D. degree in 1770 with a work entitled *De Ischiade* [Concerning Sciatica]. Shortly thereafter he went on a traveling scholarship to Paris for further study. His meeting in Amsterdam with the professors Burmann, senior and junior, men very devoted to Linnaeus, determined his further career. They assisted him, evidently after consulting Linnaeus, in getting an appointment as naturalist for an expedition on behalf of the Dutch East India Company to its overseas properties. In 1771 Thunberg went to Capetown and from there carried out several long expeditions to the interior. His fruitful studies in South Africa continued for almost five years; the literary results were *Prodromus plantarum Capensium* [Preliminary Survey of Cape Colony Plants] (published 1794–1800) and *Flora Capensis* [Cape Colony Flora] (1823), completed by J. A. Schultes. Thunberg then went on to Java early in 1775 and a few weeks after his arrival he joined a diplomatic mission of the Dutch East India Company to Japan. In that country, as a foreigner and particularly as a naturalist, Thunberg found himself in very peculiar circumstances. Freedom of movement was much restricted, and he could only botanize secretly. However, he became acquainted with some Japanese doctors to whom he gave instruction in botany and in Linnaeus's system of taxonomy. Thunberg also introduced the treatment of syphilis with quicksilver into Japan, where he spent sixteen months altogether. His return journey was by way of Batavia and Ceylon, where he devoted half a year to studying the flora, before proceeding to Holland and England and then to Sweden, after an absence of nine years. In 1781 Thunberg was named assistant professor at Uppsala; in 1784 he was appointed to his teacher's chair as successor to Linnaeus the younger. In the same year Thunberg's *Flora*

Japonica, the classic work on the flora of Japan, appeared. A few years later his travel journal was published.

The striking thing about Thunberg's work is its detachment, his interest in nature being purely scientific. He did not seek adventure in his travels and does not seem to have been especially moved by the beauty of foreign landscapes, the characteristics of new plants, or the thrill of discovery. He put the practical usefulness of plants first, observing strange and unknown landscapes and their inhabitants with impartial objectivity. Honored and respected, he lived to a ripe old age as an exemplary academic teacher in Uppsala, devoting all his spare energy to the Botanical Garden and to his museum. He retained his professorship at Uppsala until his death on August 8, 1828, at the age of eighty-six. Among Linnaeus's pupils he was survived only by Adam Afzelius, who lived until 1837 and was the first to edit the autobiographical writings of his great teacher.

REFERENCE NOTES
CHRONOLOGY
FOR FURTHER READING
INDEX

Reference Notes

Part One: THE MAN

1. FAMILY AND CHILDHOOD

   1. Carolus Linnaeus, *Vita Caroli Linnaei*, Carolus Linnaeus's Autobiography, edited by Elis Malmeström (Stockholm, Uggla, 1957), III, 90. (Further references to this work are cited as *Vita*.)
   2. *Ibid.*
   3. *Ibid.*
   4. *Ibid.*, III, 91.
   5. *Ibid.*

2. STUDIES AT LUND AND UPPSALA

   1. Quoted in T. M. Fries, *Linné, Lefnadsteckning* (2 vols. Stockholm, 1903), I, 31.
   2. Carolus Linnaeus, *Ungdomsresor*, edited by Knut Hagberg (Stockholm, 1929), *I. Iter Lapponicum*, foreword, 15 ff.

3. SOJOURN IN HOLLAND

   1. In the possession of the Linnaean Society of London. Unless otherwise identified, all quotations in this chapter are from this diary.

2. Adam Afzelius, ed., *Egenhändiga anteckningar af Carl Linnae-us* . . . (Stockholm, 1823), 32 ff.
3. *Vita*, III, 112.

4. MEDICAL PRACTICE IN STOCKHOLM

1. Quoted in Otto E. A. Hjelt, "Carl v. Linné als Arzt und medi-zinscher Schriftsteller," in *Carl von Linnés Bedeutung als Naturforscher und Arzt* (German translation of 2nd Swedish ed.; Jena, Gustav Fischer, 1909), 14.
2. Cf. *Vita*, III, 113.
3. Cf. *Vita*, III, 114.
4. Letter of January 21, 1740, quoted in Hjelt, *op. cit.*, 11 ff.
5. To C. F. Mennander, March 30, 1737, quoted in Hjelt, *op. cit.*, 12.

5. UPPSALA, 1741–1778

1. Quoted in Hjelt, *op. cit.*, 19.
2. Letter to Sauvages, May 14, 1741, quoted in Hjelt, *op. cit.*, 21.
3. Cf. *Vita*, III, 120.
4. *Vita*, III, 123.
5. Letter dated August 6, 1751, *Bref och skrivelser af ach till Carl v. Linné*, edited by J. M. Hulth (Uppsala and Berlin, 1907–1917), I, 4, 281 ff. (footnote). (Further references to this work are cited as *Bref.*)
6. Letter dated February 5, 1753, *Bref*, I, 4, 198 ff.
7. Cf. *Vita*, III, 124.
8. *Vita*, III, 124.
9. Letters dated March 20, 1761, and April 1, 1764; quoted in Hjelt, *op. cit.*, 28.
10. Johann Beckmann, *Schwedische Reise in den Jahren 1765–1766*, edited by T. M. Fries (Uppsala, 1911).
11. *Vita*, III, 124.

6. THE FINAL YEARS

1. *Vita*, III, 127.
2. Linnaeus discussed the treatment of gout in letters to Sauvages in 1753, 1754, and 1762; cf. Hjelt, *op. cit.*, 134.
3. *Vita*, III, 123.
4. Afzelius, *op. cit.*, 256.

7. PERSONALITY AND IMAGE

1. Elis Malmeström, "Linnes självkänsla," *Svenska Linné-sällskapets årsskrift (SLÅ)*, 10 (1927), 84–89.
2. Knut Hagberg, *Carl Linnaeus* (Stockholm, 1939).
3. Afzelius, *op. cit.*, 89 ff.
4. Cf. P. H. Jespersen, "J. C. Fabricius as an Evolutionist," *SLÅ* 29 (1946), 35–36.
5. Quoted in Dietrich Stoever, *Leben des Ritters Carl v. Linné* (Hamburg, 1792), II, 82.
6. Stoever, *op. cit.*, II, 98–101, 103.
7. Elis Malmeström, "Carl von Linne," *SLÅ* 31 (1948), 40.
8. Dated February 2, 1753, *Bref*, I, 4, 199 ff.
9. *Bref*, I, 5, 5 (letter of January 12, 1756); 37 (letter of January 1, 1758); 214 (letter of January 1, 1774), 235 ff (letter of January 1, 1776); others.
10. *Ibid.*, I, 4, 77; dated September 23, 1748.
11. *Ibid.*, I, 5, 80; dated December 6, 1748.
12. *Ibid.*, I, 5, 41; dated February 10, 1758.
13. Malmeström, "Linnés självkänsla," *op. cit.*, 84–98.
14. *Bref*, I, 5, 34–37.
15. *Vita*, III, 146 ff.
16. Cf. Heinz Goerke, *Die deutsch-schwedischen Beziehungen in der Medizin des 18. Jahr hunderts* (Copenhagen, 1958), 125.
17. Oscar Levertin, *Carl von Linné* (Stockholm, 1906), 38.
18. Carolus Linnaeus, *Dalaresa (Iter Dalekarlicum)*, (Stockholm, 1960), 151.
19. *Vita*, III, 145.
20. Elis Malmeström, "Linnes religiosa åskådning," *SLÅ* 5 (1922), 1–12.
21. Beckmann, *op. cit.*, 104.
22. *Ibid.*, 104 ff.
23. Cf. Beckman, *op. cit.*, 112 ff.
24. E. Ehnmark, "Linnés Nemesis-tankar och svensk folktro," *SLÅ* 24 (1941), 29–63.

Part Two: CAREER AND INFLUENCE

8. "GOD'S REGISTRAR"

1. Adolf Koelsch, in the title of an article in *Deutsche Allgemeine Zeitung*, 1928.

2. *Vita*, III, 145.

3. Cf. Erik Nordenskiöld, *Biologins historia* (Stockholm, 1925), II, 104.

4. Otto Keller, *Die antike Tierwelt* (Leipzig, 1909), 1 ff.

5. Quoted in Karl F. W. Jessen, *Botanik der Gegenwart und Vorzeit* (Leipzig, 1864).

6. *Vita*, II, 64.

7. Cf. Carolus Linnaeus, *Classes plantarum* (Leiden, 1738), 487.

8. Cf. C. A. M. Lindman, "Carl v. Linné als botanischer Forscher und Schriftsteller," in *Carl von Linnés Bedeutung . . .*, *op. cit.*, 23 ff.

9. Letter dated November 6, 1769, in the collection of letters in the Uppsala University Library, G 152.

10. Carolus Linnaeus, *Systema naturae* (Leiden, 1735), Observation 15.

11. Felix Bryk, *Linnaeus im Auslande* (Stockholm, 1919).

12. For evidence concerning the printings and translations of *Systema naturae*, see the bibliographies by J. M. Hulth (Uppsala, 1907), Emil Lindell (Växjo, 1933), Nils Sandberg and Willy Heimann (Stockholm, 1957), and especially that by B. H. Soulsby (2nd ed. London, 1933).

13. *Systema naturae;* presentation adapted from Friedrich Dannemann, *Die Naturwissenschaften in ihrer Entwicklung und in ihrem Zusammenhang* (Leipzig and Berlin, 1910–1913), 63–65.

14. Carolus Linnaeus, *Fundamenta botanica* (Amsterdam, 1736), 18, no. 156.

15. *Vita*, III, 151.

16. *Bref*, I 5, 103; dated October 6, 1762.

17. *Systema naturae*, 10th ed., *I. Animalia* (Stockholm, 1758).

18. Cf. H. S. Sjögren, "Carl von Linné als Mineralog," in *Carl von Linnés Bedeutung . . .*, *op. cit.*, 34 ff., and Paul von Groth, *Entwicklungschichte der Mineralogischen Wissenschaften* (Berlin, 1926), 151 ff.

19. Cf. Wilhelm Karst, "Zur Geschichte der 'Natürlichen Krankheitssysteme,'" *Abhandlungen zur Geschichte der Medizin und der Naturwissenschaften*, 37 (1941).

20. William T. Stearn, "An Introduction to the *Species plantarum* and Cognate Botanical Works of Carl Linnaeus," in *Carl Linnaeus, Species plantarum, a facsimile of the first edition 1753* (2 vols., London: The John Ray Society, 1957–1959).

9. INVESTIGATOR OF NATURE

1. Fries, *op. cit.*, II, 439–441.
2. *Ibid.*, 440 ff.
3. Lindman, *op. cit.*, 156–163.
4. G. Drake, "Linnés försök till in hemsk teodling," *SLÅ* 10 (1927), 68–83, and "Linnés avhandling Potus Theae 1765," *SLÅ* 22 (1939), 27–43.
5. *Bref*, I 6, 9 ff.; letter dated August 18, 1763.
6. *Vita*, III, 129 ff.
7. N. Hylander, "Om Kvickrotens nytta," *SLÅ* 30 (1947), 43–60.
8. *Vita*, III, 157.
9. Einar Lönnberg, "Carl v. Linné und die Lehre von den Wirbeltieren," in *Carl von Linnés Bedeutung . . .*, *op. cit.*, 45.
10. *Vita*, III, 129; G. Drake, "Linné och par lodlingen," *SLÅ* 13 (1930), 109–123.

10. PHYSICIAN AND TEACHER OF MEDICINE

1. *Vita*, IV, 162–165.
2. Hjelt, *op. cit.*, 22, footnote 1.
3. Quoted in Hjelt, *op. cit.*, 95; dated March 20, 1755.
4. *Bref*, I 5, 313–317.
5. *Ibid.*, I 4, 90 ff; dated October 23, 1749.
6. *Ibid.*, I 5, 203 ff.
7. *Vita*, III, 131.
8. Hjelt, *op. cit.*, 50 ff.
9. A. H. Uggla, "Linnés tankar om den akademiska ungdomens uppfostran," *SLÅ* 23 (1940), 1–16.

11. TRAVELER AND ETHNOLOGIST

1. Carolus Linnaeus, *Reisen durch Westgotland 1746*, translated by J. C. D. Schreber (Halle, 1765), 318.
2. *Ibid.*, 166.
3. *Ibid.*, 236, ff.
4. Carolus Linnaeus, *Skånsa resa 1749*, edited by C. O. von Sydow (Stockholm, 1959), 189.
5. Carolus Linnaeus, *Gotländska resa 1741*, edited by B. Mode and Knut Hagberg (2nd ed. Stockholm, 1958), 108.
6. Linnaeus, *Reisen durch Westgotland*, *op. cit.*, 249 ff.
7. Linnaeus, *Dalaresa*, *op. cit.*, 134.

8. *Ibid.*, 28 ff.
9. Linnaeus, *Reisen durch Westgotland, op cit.*, 115–117.
10. *Ibid.*, 157–159.

12. FRIENDS AND FOES

1. *Bref*, I 4, 310; dated October 15, 1754.
2. Cf. Johann Georg Zimmermann, *Das Leben des Herrn von Haller* (Zürich, 1755), 181.
3. Correspondence of J. A. Murray with Linnaeus, letter of September 21, 1769; cf. Goerke, *op. cit.*, 145.
4. Correspondence of Linnaeus with J. A. Murray; letter of October 4, 1769; cf. Goerke, *op. cit.*, 146.
5. Quoted in K. Wein, "F. Ehrhart und J. A. Murray, Zwei Typen der Botaniker der Aufklärungszeit," *SLÅ* 14 (1931), 73.
6. Cf. N. von Hofsten, "Linné och Goethe," *SLÅ* 46 (1963), 1–14.

13. CONCERNING THE "APOSTLES"

1. Carolus Linnaeus, *Critica botanica* (Leyden, 1737), 82.
2. *Bref*, I 4, 75; dated June 3, 1748.
3. *Vita*, III, 122.
4. Letter to Bäck, May 28, 1751, *Bref*, I 4, 148.

Chronology

1707   May 23 (13), Carolus Linnaeus born in Råshult in Småland.

1717   Enters elementary school in Växjö.

1724   Admitted to the secondary school in Växjö.

1727   Matriculates at the university at Lund.

1728   Continues studies at the University of Uppsala.

1730   *Praeludia sponsaliorum plantarum* [Prelude to the Betrothal of Plants]. Named lecturer in botany at Uppsala.
Begins the great botanical works *Bibliotheca botanica* [Botantical Dictionary], *Classes plantarum* [Classes of Plants], *Critica botanica* [Botanical Criticism], *Genera plantarum* [Genera of Plants].

1732   Journey through Lapland and Finland.

1733   Gives first course in chemical experimentation at Uppsala.

1734   Journey through Dalecarlia.

1735   Goes abroad. Visits Lübeck, Hamburg, Amsterdam.
June 12. Receives M. D. degree in Harderwijk.
Stay in Leyden.
September. Becomes overseer of the private botanical and zoological garden of George Clifford in Hartekamp.

1736   *Systema naturae* [System of Nature] (Leyden).
Journey to England.
Bibliotheca botanica (Amsterdam).

165

Fundamenta botanica [Fundamentals of Botany] (Amsterdam).

Musa Cliffortiana florens Hartecampi [Clifford's Flowering Banana at Hartekamp] (Leyden).

1737   October. Leaves Hartekamp. Amsterdam, Leyden.
Critica botanica (Leyden).
Flora Lapponica [Flora of Lapland] (Amsterdam).
Genera plantarum (Leyden).

1738   *Hortus Cliffortianus* [The Clifford Garden] (Amsterdam).
Early summer. Departs from Holland. Visits Antwerp, Paris. Returns to Sweden by sea.
September. Begins practice as a physician in Stockholm.
Classes plantarum (Leyden).

1739   Becomes acquainted with Carl Gustav Tessin.
May. Named physician to the Admiralty. Lectures in botany and mineralogy on commission from the mining corporation. President of the newly founded Academy of Sciences.
June 26. Marriage to Sara Elisabeth Moraea.

1740   *Systema naturae*, 2nd edition (Stockholm).

1741   Professor of theoretical and practical medicine at Uppsala.
Journey to Öland and Gotland.

1742   Exchange of departments with Rosén.
Given supervision of the Botanical Gardens.

1744   Secretary of the Royal Society of Sciences in Uppsala.

1745   Opening of a natural-history museum in the orangery building.
Ölandska och Gothländska resa 1741 [Journey to Öland and Gotland] (Stockholm and Uppsala).
Flora suecia [Flora of Sweden] (Stockholm).

1746   June–August. Trip through Västergötland.
Fauna suecia [Fauna of Sweden] (Stockholm).

1747   Named Archiater.
Wästgöta-resa 1746 [Västergötland Journey] (Stockholm).

1748   Signs of psychic depression.
Hortus Upsaliensis [The Garden of Uppsala] (Stockholm).

1749   April–August. Journey through Skåne
Materia medica (Stockholm).
Rector of the University of Uppsala.

1751   *Philosophica botanica* [Botanical Philosophy] (Stockholm).
Skånska resa 1749 [Journey through Skåne] (Stockholm).

1752   Knight of the Order of the Polar Star.

1753   *Museum Tessinianum* [The Tessin Museum] (Stockholm).
       Species plantarum [Species of Plants] (Stockholm).
1754   *Museum Adolphi Friderici* [The Museum of Adolphus Fred-
       erick] (Stockholm).
1758   Buys country estate at Hammarby, near Uppsala.
       Systema naturae, Animalia, 10th edition (Stockholm).
1759   Rector of the university.
       Systema naturae, Vegetabilia, 10th edition (Stockholm).
1762   Raised to the nobility under the name "von Linné."
1763   *Genera morborum* [Kinds of Diseases].
       Relieved of teaching obligations; son designated as his
       successor.
1764   *Museum Ludovicae Ulricae Reginae* [Museum of Queen
       Louisa Ulrica] (Stockholm).
1766   *Clavis medicinae* [Key to Medicine] (Stockholm).
       Systema naturae, 12th edition, Part I (Stockholm).
1767   *Systema naturae,* 12th edition, Part II (Stockholm).
1768   *Systema naturae,* 12th edition, Part III (Stockholm).
1772   Rector of the university.
1774   First stroke.
       Systema vegetabilium [Classification of Plants], edited by
       Johann Andreas Murray (Göttingen and Gotha).
1775   Portrait painted by Alexander Roslin.
1776   Second stroke, with permanent lameness.
1777   Chair at the university taken over by his son.
1778   January 10. Dies in Uppsala.

For Further Reading

Blunt, Wilfrid. *The Compleat Naturalist; A Life of Linnaeus.* New York, The Viking Press, 1971.

Comprehensive well-written biography; numerous illustrations. Appendix, "Linnaean Classification, Nomenclature, and Method," by William T. Stearn.

Bryk, Felix, ed. *Linnaeus im Auslande.* Stockholm, privately printed, 1919. (In German.)

Deals with the period from 1732–1738; contains Linnaeus's notes of his foreign travels; German translation of an unfinished manuscript of his foreign journey; facsimile reproductions of his articles in the *Hamburgische Berichte;* his diary of 1735; and an "autograph book" with his curriculum vitae, written by Johann Browallius, and inscriptions by important individuals. Extensive introduction, bibliography.

Carl von Linnés Bedeutung als Naturforscher und Arzt. Jena: Gustav Fischer, 1909. (German translation of the 2nd ed. of the Swedish collection of essays *Carl von Linné såsom läkare och medicinsk författare.* Uppsala, 1907.)

Six essays by various authors, discussing Linnaeus's contribution and influence in medicine, zoology (the study of vertebrates and entomology), botany, geology, and mineralogy.

Fries, T. M. *Linné, lefnadsteckning.* 2 vols. Stockholm: Fahlerantz & Co., 1903. (In Swedish.)

The basic biography of Linnaeus. *See* Jackson, Benjamin Daydon.

Gourlie, Norah. *The Prince of Botanists: Carl Linnaeus.* London: Witherby, 1953.

Hagberg, Knut. *Carl Linnaeus.* Stockholm, 1939, new ed., Natur och Kultur, 1957; English translation, London: Jonathan Cape, 1952.

Brief biography; emphasis is on Linnaeus's thought and scientific contributions and their impact on his contemporaries and successors.

Jackson, Benjamin Daydon. *Linnaeus (afterwards Carl von Linné): The Story of His Life, adapted from the Swedish of Theodor Magnus Fries.* London: Witherby, 1923.

Condensed from Fries's two-volume work, with some new material added; appendix contains a list of autobiographies; genealogies; a list of Linnaeus's students; an extract from the *Nemesis Divina;* a table explaining Swedish titles, money, and measures; a brief history of Sweden during Linnaeus's lifetime; and a selected bibliography.

Smith, James Edward. *A Selection of the Correspondence of Linnaeus and Other Naturalists.* 2 vols. London: Longman, Hurst, Rees, Orme, & Brown, 1821.

Includes short biographies of Peter Collinson, John Ellis, Alexander Garden, Daniel Solander, Johann Jakob Dillenius, and José Celestino Mutis, as well as letters from and to others.

Soulsby, B. H. *A Catalogue of the Works of Linnaeus (and Publications more immediately relating thereto) preserved in the libraries of the British Museum (Bloomsbury) and the British Museum (Natural History) (South Kensington).* London: Printed by order of the Trustees of the British Museum, Oxford University Press, 1933.

The standard reference for Linnaean publications.

Stafleu, Frans A. *Linnaeus and the Linnaeans. The Spreading of Their Ideas in Systematic Botany.* Utrecht: Oosthoek, 1971.

Part I includes a brief biography of Linnaeus and discussion of his ideas and theories, nomenclature, collections, and systems; part II deals with his students and his influence in the botanical world of western Europe.

Stearn, William T. "An Introduction to the *Species plantarum* and Cognate Botanical Works of Carl Linnaeus," in *Carl Linnaeus,*

Species plantarum, a facsimile of the first edition 1753. 2 vols. London: The Ray Society, 1957–1959.
Discussion of the botanical works that led up to the *Species plantarum*, of the sexual system, of binomial nomenclature, of the influence of the *Species plantarum* in British botany, of the Linnaean herbaria and those consulted by Linnaeus; bibliography. Excellent summary of the evolution and impact of Linnaean nomenclature.

Index

About the Author

Heinz Goerke is a medical historian and the Director of the Institute for the History of Medicine at the Free University of Berlin. He has spent many years in Sweden, is well versed in the Swedish language, and is the author of a number of works on the history of medicine and natural science in that country in the eighteenth century.